Dr Jane Williams is Assistant Dean and Lecturer in Systematic Theology at St Mellitus College, of which she is a founder member. She is the author of several books, including *Approaching Christmas* (Lion, 2005), *Approaching Easter* (Lion, 2006), *Lectionary Reflections Years A, B & C* (SPCK, 2011), *Faces of Christ* (Lion, 2011) and *Why Did Jesus Have to Die?* (SPCK, 2016). She is a regular contributor to the Church House Lectionary Reflections for Daily Prayer. She and the other founders of St Mellitus College, Bishop Graham Tomlin and the Revd Dr Michael Lloyd, appear in a regular theological podcast, Godpod. Jane has also contributed to Radio 4's *Something Understood.*

The Art of Advent

A painting a day from Advent to Epiphany

Jane Williams

First published in Great Britain in 2018

Society for Promoting Christian Knowledge
36 Causton Street
London SW1P 4ST
www.spck.org.uk

British Library Cataloguing-in-Publication Data
A catalogue record for this book is available from the British Library

ISBN 978–0–281–07169–2
eBook ISBN 978–0–281–07170–8

1 3 5 7 9 10 8 6 4 2

Typeset by Fakenham Prepress Solutions, Fakenham, Norfolk NR21 8NL
First printed in Great Britain by Micropress

eBook by Fakenham Prepress Solutions, Fakenham, Norfolk NR21 8NL

Produced on paper from sustainable forests

CONTENTS

FOREWORD

I greatly rejoice with thanksgiving for all the help I have received over the years – especially from writers and holy people, full of wisdom and insight – that has deepened my trust in God's love and friendliness and has made me see more clearly what that loving relationship invites me to be.

Jane Williams' book, *The Art of Advent*, does just that. Using 37 carefully chosen paintings with accompanying texts, she takes us on an Advent journey which challenges us to think more deeply about what we believe, why, and how it affects and influences our lives.

Starting with the great Advent themes of light and darkness, the Four Last Things and the Advent invitation, the text explores the biblical events of Advent, the birth of Christ and Epiphanytide.

The author shows how certain paintings can help us to understand different aspects of our most holy faith, often in surprising ways. We look at how a painting by Dürer helps us to see Advent not as a time for fear, but as a season when we learn to long for God. We are prompted to reflect with wisdom and insight on our lives by the exploration of a painting by Bosch and of how the choices which we make have eternal consequences.

We are also encouraged to reflect unhurriedly on what God's mighty acts in Holy Scripture, and especially in the life of Jesus of Nazareth, mean in practical terms, through searching questions after the text on each painting. These questions help us to face often difficult and uncomfortable truths of revelation which we often try to avoid, such as death being, not the end, but life in God; and why we are so afraid of it. They also help us to see how we can use Advent creatively to be the agent of transformation. I found that the prayer at the end of each chapter prompted my heart to ring with joy and delight in God.

Jane Williams has also included questions which lead us to explore how, as ambassadors of the kingdom of heaven, we may serve our mission units and neighbourhoods more faithfully as disciples of Jesus Christ – serving the poor and vulnerable, witnessing to our loving and faithful God and developing our Christian discipleship. As such, the book provides a brilliant foundation for parish and small-group discussions both during Advent and throughout the year. Wake up! Clean up! Get ready! Feed up! Grow up!

The Most Revd and Rt Hon. Dr John Sentamu
Archbishop of York

The Art of Advent

1
Light and dark

In Advent, we are preparing our hearts and our lives for the birth of Jesus. Some of this preparation will be joyful but, as with any new birth, there will also be apprehension: this new birth, more than any, is life-changing, world-changing. John's Gospel speaks of Jesus' birth as the coming of the light (John 1.2), without which nothing can live, but also in which nothing can hide.

Blake's *The Ancient of Days* shows God leaning out from the sphere of light which is God's home to begin to measure out creation. Light is symbolic of all that is God: it is life, it is truth, it is warmth, it is active, it pushes darkness away. Blake shows us all of this with superb economy. This was one of Blake's favourite images, and he used it in several different forms. The phrase 'Ancient of Days' or 'Ancient One' comes from Daniel 7 (vv. 9, 13, 22), and describes a strange, dense vision, piling detail upon detail, and combining hope and judgement in equal measure, in a way that strongly echoes our Advent themes. As God measures out the shape of the world in the picture, God is also 'measuring' the world in other ways. The extended compass is not just setting up boundaries, but also, perhaps, checking if the world is reaching its full potential, fulfilling its calling. We are watching both birth and death in Blake's picture, as we are at the cradle of the one born to die for our sins.

Blake helps us to see what Daniel meant by the phrase. This is no old man, but a timeless one, both aged and yet full of vitality. God is older than time, more 'ancient' than any human thought or life. The white hair streams in the force of creative

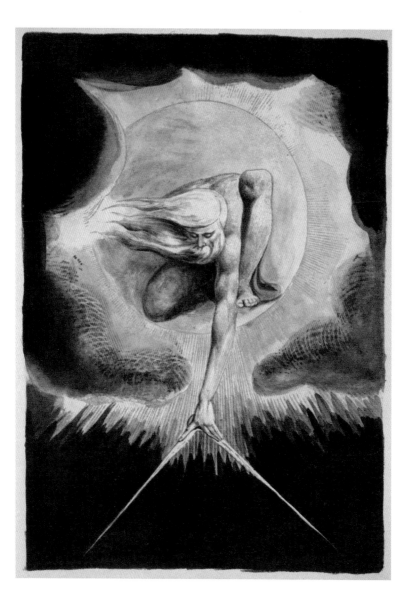

energy as the powerful figure pours out light into the chaotic
darkness around. What God begins to measure out echoes
the sphere of light behind and around the reaching figure.
The world is going to echo the dwelling place of God. See how
God's long fingers merge into one of the arms of the compass:
this is no distant creative process we are watching, but one
where the energy of God begins to light up what is being made.
The creating hand is bony, almost skeletal, as though death
is reaching up, being admitted into the divine vitality. God is
creating time, so now alongside God's own eternity there will
exist endings as well as beginnings. The very act of creation
makes that inevitable.

Most of us simply identify the 'Ancient of Days' in this picture
as God, and read into it the Genesis story of creation. We might
go further and see the Christian creation account here, as we
find it in John 1. The creating figure is human, and John tells
us that everything comes into being through the word, the one
whom we come to know in Jesus. The world will have a kind
of logic and rationality to it because it flows from the God who
chooses to be accessible to us, it flows from the Jesus-shaped
God. As we explore the world and discover more and more
about its inbuilt patterns, in mathematics, art, music, poetry,
we can see Blake's compasses at work – the creation is meant
for us to delight in and at least partially understand, say those
compasses. They are instruments that human brains and hands
will encounter.

Blake himself was more ambivalent about the interaction
of divine and human creativity. For him, this picture might
illustrate his sense that the divine is opposed to human
flourishing. He wrote: 'And Priests in black gowns, were walking

their rounds, And binding with briars, my joys & desires.' Then the reaching compasses become threatening, rather than full of potential.

Advent is a good time to face that challenge. The child who is waiting to be born demands a response. Blake's *The Ancient of Days* shows us God's own preparations for this birth, preparations that go back before time, back to the very heart and nature of God. This 'Ancient One' is full of power and purpose, shaping the world for us, but not necessarily as we might wish it to be. Jesus, through whom all things come into being, is coming to claim the world again. Is this good news, or is it terrifying?

For reflection or discussion

Are there areas of your life that you are afraid to open up to the light? If so, what can you do this Advent to prepare to let God in?

What aspects of faith have you found liberating and what have you found constricting? What can you do this Advent to make your circle more welcoming?

Lord, giver of life, creator of light, give us courage to turn to you with hope and trust. As we await the birth of your son, Jesus Christ, may the renewing Spirit teach us to trust your purposes of love, and to allow the new birth which will set us free. Amen.

2
Advent invitation

John's Gospel opens with God's perspective, starting before time. God's Advent preparations are far more all-encompassing than ours. From the start, the world has been moving towards this moment, when the light and life of the world will be born into it. But then John reminds us of the shocking reality: 'He was in the world, and the world came into being through him; yet the world did not know him' (John 1.10). It is almost like the old fairy tales, where a king disguises himself to go and live among his people and see what they really think.

But John's version is starker. God does not live in faraway luxury, ignorant of the needs of the people, because they all have their being only through the creative life of God. There is no life that is separate from God, the source of all life. So Jesus does not come on a fact-finding mission; instead, he comes with an invitation. Come home, Jesus says, come and rediscover your long-lost family, your older sibling, Jesus, and your Father, God.

This is the paradox that Holman Hunt depicts: here is the light of the world, but he is standing outside a closed door, knocking and waiting. There are few places from which all light can be wholly excluded, but this forbidding door has no keyhole, no chinks through which the waiting light can filter. It has the power to withstand the light completely, unless it is opened.

Hunt's text for the painting was Revelation 3.20: 'Listen! I am standing at the door, knocking; if you hear my voice and open the door, I will come in to you and eat with you, and you with me.' We are reminded of the encounters between Jesus and

THE LIGHT OF THE WORLD

BEHOLD I STAND AT THE DOOR AND KNOCK IF ANY MAN
HEAR MY VOICE AND OPEN THE DOOR I WILL COME
IN TO HIM AND WILL SVP WITH HIM AND HE WITH ME.

Zacchaeus (Luke 19.1–10), or the woman at the well (John 4.1–42), or the boy with the loaves and the fishes (John 6.1–14). First, people are encouraged to give out of their own resources, and then their own poor stocks are replenished from the limitless resources of God's generosity.

Holman Hunt's picture is full of symbolism, all of it taking us more deeply into Advent reflection. There are three light sources in the painting, but they all cluster around Jesus. Behind him is the dawn light, struggling to make its way through the dark woods, towards that central figure. Then there is the lantern that Jesus is carrying, a bright, homely light to welcome wandering travellers. And finally, there is the light that shines around Jesus' head, his own inner brightness, from which the other lights take their meaning. Behind Jesus are threatening, twisted trees, shedding rotting fruit to the ground. They are the tree that Adam and Eve ate from, and the tree on which Jesus died, and all our long family trees, waiting to be lit up and filled with life again. The lantern that Jesus is holding throws a reddish light back on to his cloak, which makes it look similar to the wood of the door. After all, Jesus said that he is the door or the gateway (John 10.7). So here we have two doorways, facing each other, as we wait to see whether one will open to the other.

Holman Hunt paints the crucified and risen Jesus: the marks of the nails are visible in the hand that is poised to knock, and he still wears the crown of thorns. But Jesus' willingness to be vulnerable, to lay himself open to us and await our verdict, is there from the moment of his birth. Human birth, particularly in the ancient world, is such a risky business, with no guarantee of safety, and Jesus is born to such unlikely people and is dependent on them for food, for nurture, for safety, for love.

So many things could have gone wrong at every turn of Jesus' human life; at every moment, he stands and knocks and waits for us to offer what we can, to open the door, and then the light will come streaming in.

In Advent, God does not first confront us with our sin; instead, we are invited to prepare to make God welcome; we are invited to take the initiative, to find our best selves, to be willing to open the door to the baby in need. God does not come into the world with a battering ram, but with a cry: open the door.

For reflection or discussion

What stops you opening up all the doors in your life to the invitation of God?

Do you think there are times when a battering ram works better than an invitation as an evangelistic tool?

Lord of gentle might, may we hear the patient knocking of your son, Jesus Christ, this Advent, and open all our doors to the flood of your mercy, poured out for us in the power of the Spirit. Amen.

3
Death

'Death' in *Four Horsemen of the Apocalypse*, 1511, Albrecht Dürer

Advent is not only a time of expectant looking forward. Among the themes that we are traditionally given for meditation during Advent are the 'Four Last Things' – death, judgement, hell and heaven. While these are not exactly cheering subjects, they are suitable Advent fare because they remind us that something of ultimate importance is at stake. The baby who is to be born is coming to change the world, and to offer it – and us – the choice between light and darkness, life and death.

The detail reproduced here comes from Dürer's depiction of the Four Horsemen of Revelation 6. We read that a conqueror comes, riding a white horse, to be followed by a red horse, carrying War on its back, then a black horse, whose rider measures out famine on the earth. Then, finally, comes the pale horse, ridden by Death. Its very colour is indeterminate, unlike the others that Revelation describes. It is 'greenish' or 'ashen' or 'colourless', all giving the sense that it is sickly and lifeless, wiping out colour and vitality as it goes.

Whereas the other riders brandish their weapons in front of them, Death has a trident pointing behind him, signifying his rule over the abject things following behind him. Revelation calls this Hades, the place of shadows, where the dead exist, far from God, from life, from love, from hope. So sure is Death of his reign that he does not bother to look behind him. His form is emaciated, with his bones showing through the decaying skin, and the speed of his horse makes his etiolated hair flee behind him, snarled up, unwashed, unbrushed.

The four riders move forward inexorably, looking neither right nor left, and certainly not down at what their horses are trampling underfoot. They are merciless, driven, perhaps because they know that their time is short.

Meditation on the fate of sinners, unbelievers and heretics was seen as an educational and improving device in Dürer's day. It concentrated the mind on the lasting significance of daily habits and choices. But we tend to find these warnings distasteful, with their attempts to frighten people into goodness and to terrify people into believing in the love of God. There is something counterintuitive in this for those who have been taught by Jesus that 'perfect love casts out fear' (1 John 4.18).

But in Advent, perhaps Dürer can help us not to fear but to long for God. Conquest, war and famine are an ever present reality for many in our world, and death is an inevitability for all. We are waiting for the birth of God's great saviour, but he will come as a powerless child, and will die at the hands of unjust forces. We need something deeper than optimism – we need hope. As Dürer's deathly horseman speeds on, he is not as powerful as he looks. He is driven by the knowledge of the scene against which Revelation 6 sits. The Lamb is gradually breaking the seals on the great scroll, and soon will come the time when the seventh seal is broken and a great and calm silence falls upon the heavens and the earth. So the pale horse and his rider have not got long; they are the ones who should be fearful, not us.

Perhaps the deathly rider should look back after all. In Advent, we are preparing for the coming of the one who will break death and force it to be life-giving. From where we stand, we can see Jesus harrowing hell, bringing out all those captive in the shadowlands, so that they no longer follow that imperious trident, but walk beside the saviour into freedom.

Advent is a space between two worlds. The one Dürer depicts is fearful and full of terrible power, but it is not eternal. Its meaning can and will be changed as God's new world, which is also the oldest, the original world, begins to invade. There are no armed horsemen riding to conquer, only a child, arriving like the slow, inexorable coming of the dawn. The horsemen would not even recognize God's weaponry, it is so different from their own, and that will be their downfall.

For reflection or discussion

When you think about death, what are you most afraid of?

In a world where conquest, war, famine and death still prevail, what is the difference between a message of optimism and one of hope?

Lord, we pray that you will come in judgement on a world of famine, war and death, and sow the seeds of your kingdom of peace and joy, through the mighty and tender power of the Holy Spirit, and in the name of Jesus Christ, our Lord. Amen.

4
Judgement

The Last Judgement,
c.1482, Hieronymus
Bosch

Bosch, like Dürer, was painting at a time of immense uncertainty, when there were exaggerated fears that the end of the world might be close. Bosch's wild and tortured pictures were intended as a warning and an allegory: the choices we make now have eternal consequences.

Although most of the space in this painting is taken up with depictions of what happens to those who have made the wrong choices in life, the eye is drawn to the bright, clean colour at the top of the painting. Bosch's imaginative ingenuity has created a landscape of horror, but he has smeared it over with darkness, so that we have to peer to see what is going on, whereas at the top of the picture there is clarity. The lower part of the picture makes us feel as though we are suffocating, and we long for the clean, sweet air of the blue firmament above.

In the foreground of the picture, we are shown the terrible consequences of the seven deadly sins. With sickening power, Bosch makes it clear how unappealing they are; there is nothing sensuous or attractive about the sins of the flesh in this spectacle of horror. The human forms are all mutilated and attended by demonic, semi-human figures. This is fitting company for the sinful.

The bottom third of the painting is in mud colours – ochre, brown, occasional patches of rust. The middle of the painting is darker and emptier. There is no activity here, only devastation. It looks as though there has been a great fire that has destroyed

a civilization and left a lifeless exclusion zone between the top and the bottom of the picture.

The top third is like a drink in the desert. Its background is a peculiarly sweet and piercing blue. In contrast to the scene of chaos and darkness below, here is order, calm, colour. The light and the clear lines and spheres give a sense of balance and restored perspective. Our eyes are not being dragged here and there, but allowed to rest in the peaceful lines and curves.

Jesus sits, balanced upon two arcs whose lower rims are hidden by darkness. Could this be a hint of hope in this otherwise wholly distressing painting? Do the spheres extend underneath the darkness and horror? The world that God created might be gradually, insistently reasserting itself, somewhere out of our sight, as the light from the top of the painting starts to conquer the darkness. The angels' trumpets pierce the gloom with ease. There is still the possibility of communication between these apparently separate parts of the painting.

Whether this is what Bosch thought he was painting or not, that is the point of meditating on judgement during Advent. There is still time, and God is coming to reclaim us. God's coming judgement in Jesus Christ is not designed to condemn. Instead, God comes to show us himself, the judge; and what we see is that God is for us, he comes to set us free, to invite us home. In Jesus, we see a human being whose choices are wholly determined by his relationship with the God whom he calls 'Father'. From that overriding centre, Jesus calls the people he meets into relationship, too. He heals them, forgives them, draws disparate people together to sit at his table and feast from God's bounty. This is God's judgement – he is and will be our God.

Yet we do still have a choice. The Gospels show us people who hate Jesus and reject him. Perhaps more alarmingly for most of us, they also show us people who just find Jesus irrelevant and get on with their lives as though they cannot see the choice being offered to them. We have heard God's judgement on us – 'God so loved the world that he gave his only Son' (John 3.16). Advent is a time to ponder our own judgement on ourselves. We can judge that we are fit to be God's children and sit at the table with all the family, as we are invited to do. Or we can judge that we are better off alone. Either judgement will need to be lived out, and will have eternal consequences, because these decisions will shape who we are.

For reflection or discussion

What are your 'besetting' sins, the ones you find hardest to overcome, and how do you think they are shaping the person you are becoming?

Are there constructive ways of talking about 'judgement' in our culture?

Lord, in this Advent season, lift our eyes to your mercy seat, where Jesus Christ, the Son, sits and judges us worthy to be his sisters and brothers. Give us courage to reach out in the power of the Holy Spirit and take the outstretched hand of the Son, leading us home. Amen.

5

Hell

This dwelling on the Four Last Things – death, judgement, hell and heaven – in Advent can seem morbid. Indeed, some of the ways in which it has been done in the past have undoubtedly been counterproductive and deeply out of tune with the major themes of Advent. We are preparing to welcome the birth of the Prince of Peace, Immanuel, God with us, so this constant harping on about things that undermine our sense of God's loving purpose is surely unhelpful.

But the point of this more sombre note is to remind us that we are not just preparing for an annual party, after which the world goes back to normal when the decorations are packed away. This is the decisive, pivotal moment for the whole world: its maker is coming to live in it and to change its possibilities for ever.

Bosch seems to have captured the market in strange and terrifying visions of the consequences that flow from a failure to notice that the time has come to choose our personal destiny and the fate of the world. The commonplace sins of greed, selfishness and sensuality become monstrous in his paintings, dehumanizing all who practise them. We know surprisingly little about Bosch. We have no explanation for his tortured landscapes, executed with such precision and verve. Nor do we know much about his inner religious landscape: it was probably conventional, at least outwardly, though so very far from conventional in artistic expression.

Bosch painted several triptychs, usually with Eden and Adam and Eve's first choice on one side, and the bitter fruits of that

choice in hellish detail on the other. The centre of the triptych from which this depiction of hell comes is a strange and much-debated painting of *The Garden of Earthly Delights*. What is striking about the depiction of hell reproduced here is not so much the bizarre images and the esoteric forms of torture on display as the sheer isolation of each of the figures. They do not seem to see each other, or to interact at all. Their unfocused gaze suggests that they are almost unaware of their terrible surroundings. Only the pale, hollowed-out figure in the upper left-hand corner – part fish, part tree, part human – looks out of the picture with its one visible, melancholy eye.

In *The Great Divorce*, C. S. Lewis describes 'hell' as the state we create for ourselves when we shut ourselves up in what Lewis calls 'the dungeon of [our] own mind'. Wandering in the grey town that is hell, no person truly connects with others or with anything real; they are all locked up in obsessions about themselves. In Lewis's exploration, hell is not 'real'. We can leave it whenever we choose, and then it ceases to be. But if we choose to stay there by obsessing about ourselves, our needs, the way we have been misused and wrongly judged by others who do not realize how important we are, then, Lewis suggests, 'hell' starts to seep out and into the rest of our lives, so that even things that might have been good, fruitful and life-giving are emptied of meaning and filled only with thoughts of ourselves.

Lewis's notion of hell, like Bosch's, is imaginary, but they are surely on to something in their emphasis on isolation. St Paul says that nothing 'will be able to separate us from the love of God in Christ Jesus' (Romans 8.39), and St John says that Jesus gives us 'power to become children of God (John 1.12). St Peter says, 'Once you were not a people, but now you are

God's people' (1 Peter 2.10). Jesus himself is profoundly rooted in his belonging to God, as a Son to a Father, and the prayer he teaches his followers, 'Our Father', is one that invites us into that relationship. At the Ascension, the power of that Jesus-like relating to the Father stays with us in the presence of the Holy Spirit. The heart of the universe is the dynamic, interweaving love of Father, Son and Holy Spirit, the opposite of the isolation that Bosch and Lewis depict as hell.

Perhaps that is why Jesus' cry from the cross is so shocking. In desolation, he cries out, 'My, God, my God, why have you forsaken me,' as though experiencing for the first time the hell of separation that human beings have created for themselves.

For reflection or discussion

Do you think that a description of hell as self-obsessed isolation rings true?

How can we help create a culture of relating that is good for both introverts and extroverts?

Lord, this Advent, confront us, we pray, with the hellish isolations we create for ourselves and for others, and lead us, with all your joyful people, to the heart of your great love, Father, Son and Holy Spirit. Amen.

6
Heaven

*The Return of the
Prodigal Son,*
1666–9, Rembrandt
van Rijn

Jesus tells several stories about people searching for lost things.
For example, there is a woman who loses a coin and searches
her whole house until she finds it, and then throws a party for
all her neighbours to celebrate the find (Luke 15.8–10); or there
is the shepherd who risks losing all his sheep to go in search of
the one who strayed from the flock (Matthew 18.12–14). In both
of those parables, the assumption is that the one who is doing
the searching is God. Indeed, Jesus says that his mission is 'to
seek and to save the lost' (Luke 19.10). The stories are mostly
received with some hostility by the comfortably religious people
of Jesus' day, as they probably would be by a lot of us, if we were
honest. Surely it is God's job to reward those who have not gone
off and got lost, but have faithfully attended to God and stayed
where they should be? What is the point of being a good sheep,
if God prefers the bad ones?

The parable of the prodigal son is unusual in that it is the son, the
sinful one, not the good and loving father, who does the seeking.
True, the father is described as constantly on the lookout for the
son, so he sees him coming when he is still a long way away, but
it is the son who takes the initiative in this story: he gets himself
lost, and then he comes to his senses and returns home. It is also
unusual in that the story does not stop when the lost one is found;
we also hear the older brother's feelings of hurt and rejection
because of what looks like his father's partiality for the bad boy.

Rembrandt's painting of the moment of reunion between the
father and the errant son must be one of the most reproduced

and commented upon of all paintings. Its depiction of merciful, tender, rejoicing love is unequalled. The father stoops down to embrace his filthy and disgraced son, not caring what state he is in, so long as he is safely home. The son has lost all his dignity and self-respect – look at his bare, shorn head, a sure sign that he has put himself outside the respectable circles of his religion and class; look at the engrained grime on his bare foot. If ever a human being needed help, it is him.

But the light in the picture falls on two faces: the father's and the older son's, at either side of the painting. The prodigal's face is in shadow, as though he is not really the one we are interested in. Yet, his face is turned towards his older brother, whose eyes are fixed on him. The younger brother could be mocking the older, or beseeching him – we cannot see. The older brother's face is intense and puzzled, the slight frown looking not so much angry as bewildered. There is a stillness to the picture, as though we are part way through a story whose ending we do not yet know.

And, in a sense, that is true. Jesus does not tell us how the older brother reacts when the father explains that there is enough love to go round. The older brother is not loved less because of the father's love for his younger son. It is as though Jesus leaves the story with us to make the choice.

It is tempting when thinking about heaven – the final one of the Four Last Things we are encouraged to ponder in Advent – to be over-concerned about who will be 'in' and who will be 'out'. That has been a particular hobby of Christians who feel that they have tried to live faithfully and ought to be rewarded, and it is as though the reward loses its savour if it is shared with the unrighteous. Rembrandt challenges us to see that the opposite might be true. We could join in with God's rejoicing, knowing that we have nothing to lose and everything to gain if heaven is shared. During the long absence of the prodigal son, it is not just the father who has lost something; it is also the older brother. Can he learn to rejoice that he has his brother back?

Jesus' self-definition, as the one sent to find the lost, puts a whole new complexion on heaven. Our Advent task is to see this with excitement and longing, knowing that we need our brothers and sisters if we are to be happy in heaven.

For reflection or discussion

Do you sometimes feel that God loves others more than you?

What is your understanding of 'heaven', and where do you think those ideas and images came from?

Lord, lead us this Advent into the abundance of your limitless love, and as your Holy Spirit welcomes us, may we also welcome each other, in Jesus Christ our Lord. Amen.

7

The patriarchs

Abraham, Isaac and Jacob, fifteenth century, fresco in the Orthodox rock church of Abuna Yemata Guh, Gheralta region, Tigray, Ethiopia

In Advent, as we prepare for the birth of Jesus, we are encouraged to remember that this event has been in preparation for much longer than the few weeks of Advent. The Son of God becomes incarnate, living with his people, in the birth of Jesus Christ, but God has not been distant and uninterested in the world before this. On the contrary: Jesus is the truth of the eternal character of God, who has been drawing people into relationship since creation began.

The Advent wreath is a useful way to help us remember all those who have contributed to the story we are now celebrating. Each candle in the wreath brings us a bit of the narrative, with the first candle usually commemorating the patriarchs.

Here, we see the patriarchs, Abraham, Isaac and Jacob, posed, as for a family photograph. They are in their best clothes, and the painting emphasizes the lovely flowing curves of the material of sleeves and robes. But the faces look apprehensive, reminding us of some of the family history. Isaac is born to Abraham and his wife Sarah after a visit from three mysterious strangers, whom Christian theology has always seen as a hint of the divine Trinity, subtly pointing to the fact that one day this child promised to Abraham and Sarah would be succeeded by another promised child, a still greater sign of the way in which God keeps his promises.

But between Abraham and his adult son, in this image, there is a dark secret. The story is found in Genesis 22.1–19: Isaac,

the son that Abraham and Sarah had been longing for with increasing desperation and mounting despair, has miraculously been born, just as the enigmatic visitors had promised. At last, it looks as though God's promise to Abraham – that he and his descendants will inherit the land – could really come true. And then, suddenly, God asks Abraham to take Isaac up a mountain and sacrifice him. This seems such a nonsensical command. It goes against everything that Abraham has learned about God, and seems to undermine all the trust between them. Yet Abraham sets off, without question, to give back to God the son on whom all his hopes of God's faithfulness depended. Right at the last moment, with Isaac bound and Abraham's knife drawn, God accepts that Abraham really does trust in him, and provides an alternative in the shape of a ram. No wonder Isaac stands beside Abraham with a slightly anxious expression on his face.

This is a desperately perplexing story, where God seems to test Abraham's faith mercilessly, to the point where there is no doubt in Abraham's mind that he will always trust God. Christian writers have seen this dark episode as a prefiguring of Jesus. God the Son will be the perfect sacrifice, making all other sacrifices unnecessary. His death will seem like the end of all God's faithfulness, but it will prove to be the greatest demonstration that God is always to be trusted, however things appear.

The third patriarch pictured here is Jacob, Isaac's somewhat reprehensible younger son. Jacob cheats his older brother, Esau, out of his birth right, is cheated by his father-in-law and tricks him in return, fathers a brood of quarrelsome sons, including Joseph, and generally seems far from a model citizen (see Genesis 25—35 for the whole story). Yet Jacob is also a mystic, who encounters God and never doubts what he sees and dreams.

As he runs away from the justifiable anger of Esau, Jacob makes himself an uncomfortable bed with a rock for a pillow. In his dreams he sees a ladder between heaven and earth, with angels climbing up and down. God comes and stands beside Jacob and promises that, even far from home, God can and will be present.

Abraham, Isaac and Jacob helped prepare the world to understand the action of God in Jesus. God is faithful and to be trusted, even though God seldom seems to act as we would like or expect, and even though we, like Jacob, are not always reliable partners for the divine promise and action. In Jesus Christ, God creates a way to be present with us always, a way that is far more effective than any ladder between heaven and earth.

For reflection or discussion

Are you aware that there is an area of your life where you just do not trust that God is faithful and reliable?

Who are the people who have helped prepare you to be ready to meet God?

Lord, in all the dark and testing circumstances of life, may we trust in Jesus Christ, that, in the power of his resurrection from the dead, we may find the new life of the Spirit, leading us into hope and truth. Amen.

8

Prophets

Jeremiah Lamenting the Destruction of Jerusalem, 1630, Rembrandt van Rijn

Like the patriarchs, the prophets help us prepare for the coming of Christ by maintaining an expectation of the presence and action of God. Even in situations where God seemed utterly remote or powerless, the prophets continued to hear God and to discern him at work.

Rembrandt paints Jeremiah at a moment of absolute despair. Jerusalem, the political and religious heart of the nation, has fallen to Nebuchadnezzar and his troops, and King Zedekiah, in the background of the picture, has been blinded and is about to be carried off into exile, together with most of the nobles and the educated people of the country. Jeremiah had been warning of this for so long, and now it has happened.

The vocation of a prophet is not one to be sought lightly. Jeremiah's calling set him apart from his friends and neighbours because they simply did not want to hear what God had to say through him. The words of warning and judgement that are all God will speak through Jeremiah brought him hatred, fear, isolation, death threats and imprisonment. The people blamed Jeremiah as though it was the message that was the problem, rather than their actions.

Jeremiah received his prophetic call when he was a boy, although God tells him that the vocation has been waiting for him from the moment of his conception, perhaps even before. Rembrandt shows the prophet prematurely aged by his burdensome gift, about to be carried off into exile, never

to return to his homeland. When God calls Jeremiah to be a prophet, he is under God's protection: 'I . . . have made you today a fortified city, an iron pillar, and a bronze wall, against the whole land' (Jeremiah 1.18). Now, Rembrandt shows us the effects of that promise after decades of faithfully speaking God's word to people who did not want to hear it. Jeremiah is safe and has been treated with respect by the Babylonian army, but his safety is won at the cost of all ordinary human ties. Even now, at the moment when no one can deny that Jeremiah was speaking the truth, he is still alone.

Rembrandt is a master of light and shade, so the light around Jeremiah perhaps signals something. It is not clear where the light is coming from, and it is strangely soft, almost as though it is wrapping Jeremiah in a comforting presence that he is not yet able to acknowledge. Perhaps, after all, Jeremiah is not quite as alone as he appears at first?

The great Hebrew prophets give us an example of human faithfulness that will not renounce God, come what may. This steadfastness finds its fullest expression in Jesus, who always chooses, even in the bitter garden of Gethsemane, to be the Son of his Father, and to put God first. Jeremiah knows that his relationship with God is what he was born for, and Jesus shows us that this is true for all of us. The world is son-shaped from before its conception, all of us longed into being by the love of God.

Yet Jesus, too, is met with rejection, hostility, plots and death threats. His own people doubt him and are offended by his claim to authority. This theme seems to repeat throughout human interaction with God. We will put up with a god who gives us what we want and does not demand too much of us, but we reject a God who expects to shape us, even if that might be for our own good.

The prophets bring good news, too: whatever happens, God is God and God is for us. Even Jeremiah, the darkest of prophets, has moments when he can see beyond the immediate destruction of his people to a time when they will again know that God has not abandoned them. To spend time in Advent in the company of the prophets is to open ourselves up to the great and costly truth that the world is God's and can be lived in peaceably and joyfully only by people who know who they are and whose they are. In that sense, we are all called to be prophets, in that we point to the bigger narrative of which we are a part; we point towards the action of God in Jesus Christ, and prepare ourselves to live in the world that God has made.

For reflection or discussion

Do you sometimes fear that faith in God will isolate you from others?

How might our lives 'prophesy' about God?

Lord, you know your creatures from all eternity, and have called them to you through Jesus Christ: in this Advent season, give us the grace of your Holy Spirit to take up our calling, and to prophesy to the world that it will find its fulfilment in you. Amen.

9

John the Baptist

The Virgin and Child with St Anne and St John the Baptist, c.1499– 1500, Leonardo da Vinci

John the Baptist is an obvious candidate for a candle in the Advent wreath, reminding us of God's preparations for the birth of Jesus. He is introduced in Mark's Gospel with the words from Isaiah about a messenger who is sent to prepare the way, and he himself speaks of 'the one who . . . is coming after me' (Mark 1.1–8). As Advent is a time of preparation for the birth of Jesus, there could be no better guide than John the Baptist.

Leonardo's sketch shows us a portrait of a happy family, but with clear signs that the two little boys have a destiny. The sketch is tender and intimate, but the almost sculptural tones also give a sense of strength and eternity. Sketches are usually forerunners of a painting, but this sketch of John, the forerunner in his family setting, did not lead to a painting, as far as we know. This little moment of calm stands alone.

The two women are Mary and her mother, Anne. Mary is still young enough to sit on her mother's knee, and Anne smiles at her, with affection and admiration. For Anne, at least, Mary is still the important one. But Mary and John are both looking at Jesus, who is perched on Mary's lap and clinging on to Anne's arm, as he holds up his fingers to bless John. The gesture of Anne's hand pointing upwards is one Leonardo uses several times in his paintings, to remind us of the vital if invisible presence of God. The way in which Jesus' and Anne's hands intertwine subtly reminds us of Jesus' connection with God: he is a sign of what Anne is pointing to, and his action is also God's. Although there may well be an allusion to the bigger horizon of

God's action through these two little boys, the hands also serve to hallow this lovely domestic scene. There is much still to come for John and for Jesus, including pain and death, but here, now, they are surrounded by love, both human and divine.

The lines of the sketch flow naturally and smoothly from Anne to Mary to Jesus, but John's gaze comes in from the side, from another direction. Even here, at this time of easy warmth within the family, John is very slightly removed. He leans in towards the others, but he is not cuddled in as the others are. From boyhood onwards, Leonardo suggests, John is preparing to be marginal: 'the friend of the bridegroom', John calls himself, the best man, not the groom. 'He must increase, but I must decrease' (John 3.30) is not something John comes out with suddenly but something he has been preparing for all his life.

We do not know if John was ever tempted to believe that he was more than a forerunner, or whether he was confident in his humility all along. He had reason for confidence: just like Jesus, ancient prophecies were seen to be referring to John; just like Jesus, an angel came to announce the forthcoming arrival. Like Jesus, people flocked to hear John's preaching, and he, too, attracted fascinated and terrified notice from those in power. We get no hint that John ever thought that perhaps he, and not Jesus, was the Messiah. But we do have one poignant glimpse of uncertainty. Sitting in prison and awaiting death, John sends to ask Jesus: 'Are you the one who is to come, or are we to wait for another?' (Matthew 11.3). John needs to know if his life's work is done. John's calling is to prepare for the coming of the Messiah, Jesus, but that means that he is like a gatekeeper, perpetually condemned to stand outside and point the way for others to go in.

Jesus' words about John seem harsh: 'Among those born of women there has arisen no one greater than John the Baptist. Yet the one who is least in the kingdom of heaven is greater than he' (Matthew 11.11). But this is in fact a powerful testimony to John's faithfulness; although he did not see what we can now all see – Jesus crucified, risen and ascended to the Father's right hand – he never swerved from his task of pointing the way for the rest of us.

That is why John is such a good companion in Advent. When the presence and action of God seem unclear, we can at least follow John's good example and keep looking for what is to come, and signalling its approach to others. We do not need to have all the answers ourselves; we only need to do the one thing that we are called to do, which is to point to Jesus.

For reflection or discussion

Do you love to be in the limelight, or are you able to stand aside and let others take the attention?

What can we do to point the way to Jesus?

Father of all, send us the Holy Spirit so that we may prepare the way of the Lord Jesus Christ, in our lives and in our world. Teach us to lift our eyes and look with longing hope for that day when he will return to draw all people to himself. Amen.

10
Joseph

Christ in the House
of his Parents,
1849–50, John
Everett Millais

Joseph is not one of the people regularly commemorated by a candle in the Advent wreath, but surely he should be. His role in protecting Mary and Jesus deserves our attention and meditation. Joseph sacrifices a great deal to help prepare the way for God's work of salvation in Jesus. He trusts God and he trusts Mary, against all the odds. We know very little about Jesus' childhood, but we do know that when his ministry started, people were baffled that 'the carpenter's son' could have such authority (Matthew 13.55), and we also have some evidence in the way in which Jesus spoke about the fatherhood of God to suggest that his experience of his earthly father was positive. Fathers in Jesus' stories are always allied with the action of God – think of the father of the prodigal son. Of course, Jesus' relationship with his heavenly Father is the primary interpretive focus for these stories, but the Gospels suggest that the heavenly Father took good care that Jesus should be watched over by a brave and loving earthly father too.

Millais' painting caused an outcry when it first appeared, because of the ordinariness of what he depicted. Here is a messy workshop, obviously the heart of a small family business. Jesus has just cut himself, presumably on the nail that his grandmother Anne is about to pull out of the door Joseph is working on. She will not be able to do the same for all the nails Jesus will face in his life, and Mary's extreme anxiety, as she kneels to 'kiss it better', is a glimpse of the fear that is to come. Jesus' cousin, John, is carefully carrying a bowl of water to

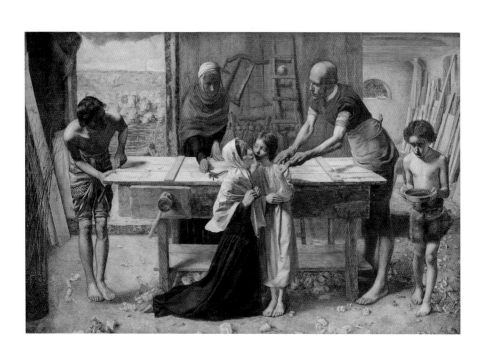

wash the wound, and that, too, is an image with a long shadow, pointing to the time when John will baptize Jesus in the Jordan. We, Jesus' followers, are represented by the sheep peering through the open doorway.

Although Jesus and Mary are at the centre of the painting, the whole setting is Joseph's. It is his carpenter's workshop, and although it is a rough-and-ready place, where a boy may come by a minor injury, it is also a place of security and family industry. Joseph is not fussing, unlike Mary, but he is concerned: look at the way his hands yearn towards the boy.

It is hard to see why critics so hated this picture when it was first shown. It is full of reverent pointers towards Jesus' ministry and teaching, but it does show real people, wearing ordinary clothes, rather than the classical, atemporal drapery of medieval paintings, and it shows ordinary human emotions. Mary is no enigmatic, peaceful beauty, and although Jesus wears a white gown, unlike the rougher garb of John and the young carpenter's assistant, he is barefoot and red-headed, both human details that critics found disturbing.

Yet it is precisely this ordinariness that Joseph provides for his little family, while he can. There is no mention of him at the foot of the cross or among the apostles in the upper room after the Ascension, although Mary is there (Acts 1.14). The tradition that Joseph was considerably older than Mary, shown in Millais' painting, may suggest that Joseph was already dead by this point. Certainly, he could not have protected Jesus from the cross, however much he might have wanted to. He could not pack him and Mary up and take them off to safety in Egypt again, as he did when the baby Jesus was threatened by Herod's anger

(Matthew 2.14). But Joseph had done his work in preserving Jesus long enough to meet this necessary, bitter end.

As an Advent companion, Joseph encourages us to discern our own part and to play it, fully. Joseph was willing to be and to do just what God needed from him, and so he assists in God's salvation of the world in Jesus. He was willing not to be centre stage, to lean in with love from the side of the picture, as Millais shows him, offering comfort but not offended if it is not needed. It is Joseph who is descended from David and so gives Jesus his family tree, his connection to the proper story of God's Messiah; it is Joseph's heritage that takes the pregnant Mary to Bethlehem for the birth of her baby. There is nothing tangential about Joseph's part in the birth of Jesus: it has been prepared for in God's long plans just as much as Mary's. Let that be a comfort to those of us who feel we are always asked to play the minor parts.

For reflection or discussion

Who has taught you most about the character of God?

What can we do to help protect and nurture the gifts and callings of others?

Lord, teach us to value the ordinary gifts of the Spirit, gifts of faithfulness, patience, kindness and self-control, and to find our life's fulfilment in serving your Son, Jesus Christ. Amen.

11
The Virgin Mary

The Annunciation, 1898, Henry Ossawa Tanner

Above all the people we walk with through Advent, there is Mary. Mary is the one who carries inside her the child we are all waiting for. Mary is the one who has said yes to God's plan of salvation, and so she makes the whole thing possible. Hers is the final candle in the outer ring of the Advent wreath.

God's preparations for this birth have gone back centuries, so it seems unlikely that Mary could have said no to the angel and subverted the whole narrative, which starts, according to John 1, even before the world comes into existence.

Yet the tender scene between Mary and the angel is a vital expression of how God's action works with us, not against us; not in competition with us, not over-ruling us, but enabling us to be who we are. Henry Ossawa Tanner shows us Mary as troubled and uncertain but looking directly into the angelic light; there is a real dialogue of respect going on here.

Mary is drawn as a young woman, barefoot, wrapped in a nightgown. The room is cramped and dingy; it looks as though she sleeps in the family's main living space, with just a screen to give her some privacy. The light could almost be the sun breaking through, except that this sun is coming through a wall, not a window. The angel is not the usual semi-human figure with wings, but a bolt of pure energy, which makes us wonder how the angelic visitor is communicating. However Mary hears what is said, she does not look terrified, merely anxious. There must be a gentleness in the angel's approach, as well as a quiet self-possession in Mary's response.

This moment is going to have to sustain Mary through the lonely and difficult times ahead. There is the shape of a shelf behind the angel's lighted shoulders, making the outline of a cross; there is no false bargain here, no promise that all will be plain sailing. When, in later years, Mary doubts, as she surely must have done, there will be no one who can remind her of what she heard and said; she is quite alone with the angel. It is striking that Mary asks for no promises for herself, she simply seeks assurance that angels know how human babies come into existence, and then she says, 'Yes.'

In her song of praise, the Magnificat (Luke 1.46–55), Mary describes the character of this God, who is able and willing to make a simple girl the cornerstone of the mighty plan for salvation. But we can also hear God singing Mary's praise in these words. Here is a young girl who understands God well enough to believe and trust in what he asks of her. Here is the character of God responding to the character of Mary, just as much as the other way round.

For each of us, this is the daily advice Mary gives us through Advent. Mary does not become less herself by responding to God. God's plan, beginning with the creation of the world, is not in danger of being derailed by Mary because God knows Mary so well. God's knowledge does not take away her freedom and turn her into an automaton, any more than our knowledge of the people we love does. We may have complete certainty about what our dearest friends will choose, not because we are forcing them to, but because it is so characteristic of them. When we throw in our lot with God's plan, we can be certain that we will play the part that is perfect for us. When we struggle to assert ourselves in opposition to God, we are struggling against what sets us free to be ourselves.

That is not to say that our lives will be all sweetness and light in the service of God, as Mary's path makes plain. This is the journey that will mean that 'all generations call her blessed', but there must have been times when she longed for peaceful obscurity, even if that meant denying her truest self.

Advent prepares us for the reality that there is only one story of the world, only one destiny for it, from before all time, and that is for it to find its fulfilment through the Son of God. We can choose not to be involved in telling the world its story, but we cannot choose to make another story the true one, because we are not God.

For reflection or discussion

What are you most afraid that God might ask you to be or do?

Do you think it is true that you can be completely known by God and completely free?

Lord, you have known us from our mother's womb: as we seek you in the face of Jesus Christ, give us your Holy Spirit to lead us daily more deeply into the freedom and joy that only you can give. Amen.

12
The Christ Child

The Holy Family with St Mary Magdalen, c.1590–5, El Greco

The final candle in the Advent wreath stands, of course, for Jesus, the light of the world. This candle is lit for the first service of Christmas and, according to John 1's creation theology, this candle has more preparation behind it than any of the others. Before the world came into existence, it was already heading towards finding its truth in Jesus.

El Greco painted several variations on the Holy Family, most of them with this very recognisable heart-shaped structure, with Mary and the child at the centre and two others leaning in from the side. Here, it is Joseph on one side and Mary Magdalene on the other, which is unusual. The New Testament does not suggest that Mary Magdalene knew Jesus' family, although we do read about a certain level of companionship among the women disciples and Jesus' mother at the time of his crucifixion and then again at the resurrection. But El Greco is probably not alluding to some unwritten tale about Mary Magdalene; he is simply using all that she has come to stand for in Christian theology to bring a poignancy to this painting. Notice that her face is shadowed, her hood partly obscuring it, and even her hand on the Virgin's shoulder is in partial darkness. She stands for the sinners for whom Jesus is born to die.

Joseph is quite cheerfully offering Jesus a bowl of fruit, with little sign of any deeper knowledge in his face. But the Virgin's hand is hovering over a small and wizened apple: it is not clear if she is giving it to Jesus or trying to take it away – perhaps both. For this is the eternal apple, from the garden of Eden, the apple that

symbolizes the continuing human choice to go our own way, against God's good desires for us. Mary Magdalene knows the sickness brought by this apple in her own life, and also knows that Jesus has the remedy. She leans, trustingly, on the Virgin's shoulder, but her shadowed, downcast face suggests that she knows the pain that Mary is feeling, as she gazes out of the picture, with a certain stern sadness.

The Child Jesus seems completely at ease. He is shown not as a baby but as a lively toddler, who seems about to jump off his mother's knee as soon as he has grasped the fruit. No one is forcing this apple into his hand; he could have taken his pick from the bowl Joseph is holding out, but he has chosen the apple, and his sturdy little legs and shiny hair suggest a radiant health and happiness about his choice. Jesus is able and willing to take up the task for which he was born.

The painting perpetuates the besmirching of Mary Magdalene's name; she becomes the famous fallen woman through a careless amalgamation of gospel stories about women with ointment and women called Mary. But the only thing we are told for certain is that her life was turned around by her encounter with Jesus, who healed her of 'seven devils' (Mark 16.9). However her story is told, she knew the weight of a fallen world, and the liberation that Jesus brings.

El Greco helps us to see Advent as a time of preparing for freedom. The coming of Jesus is the triumphant entry of the world's king, come to throw out the occupying forces. But when God acted through Moses to free the children of Israel and bring them out of slavery in Egypt, after the initial excitement of victory, walking through the Red Sea while God held the waves back like a mother parting the long grass for a toddler, the people realized that freedom is hard work. In the wilderness years, the people have to learn to be free, to trust God, to take care of each other, to hope and keep walking forward. All the years of slavery, when they had no choice, no decisions to make, have left their mark. Freedom is not easy, as Mary Magdalene found when she was sent to tell the other disciples that Jesus is risen from the dead.

In Advent, one of the things we are doing is preparing to live in our freedom as God's redeemed people, and that means facing our fears about what will be required of us if we truly have hope and choice. The Christ Child in El Greco's painting reaches out freely, eagerly, to do what is necessary, and, in Advent, we are preparing to follow his example, with hope and courage, knowing that we are no longer enslaved but free.

For reflection or discussion

Are there habits that you know you need to break if you are to be truly free?

What are the signs that we are not yet at ease with our freedom, but continue to live as though we are enslaved?

Lord Jesus Christ, you came in freedom and love to redeem your people: teach us to accept this great gift with joy, and fill us with the Holy Spirit so that we, too, may live not as slaves but as your brothers and sisters, children of the same Father. Amen.

13

Watching
and waiting:
the angels

The Nativity,
1470–5, Piero della
Francesca

Angels frame Advent. An angel announces to Zechariah that
he and his wife, Elizabeth, are to have a baby who will prepare
the way for the coming Messiah. Gabriel is rather fierce, but
that is at least partly Zechariah's own fault. Zechariah is doing
his inherited duty in the Temple and should be at home in the
presence of an angel, but instead he is terrified and doubting
and is struck dumb for his faithlessness. He has to wait the
nine months until the birth of his son, John the Baptist, to
recover his speech (Luke 1). In contrast, Gabriel's visit to Mary
is gentle and respectful, in response to Mary's courage and
faith.

Angels return, in numbers, for the birth of Jesus. Mysteriously,
the full glory of the angelic host's announcement is directed to
a group of shepherds, so that they can make their way to the
cradle of the Messiah (Luke 2.8–14). Luke does not explain why
the shepherds are the appropriate people to hear the paean of
praise with which the angels sing about the glorious thing that
God is doing. The shepherds prove their worth by getting up and
doing what the angels have told them to do – they go to see the
child, laid in a manger.

Piero della Francesca has brought the angels to worship at the
manger with the shepherds. This is a scene of perfect rejoicing
and praise. The angels are playing and singing, and it looks as
though the figures behind Mary are joining in, including the ox.
The baby is waving his arms in time to the music, and kicking
his chubby little legs, lying on his little bit of what looks like the

blue, blue sky. Only Mary's adoration is too deep for words, as she gazes on the wonder she has helped bring into the world.

The setting is homely, even ramshackle, with a familiar town landscape in the background and a sagging little stable sheltering the figures, yet the scene is full of the praise of heaven and earth. Any setting, anywhere, is appropriate to the worship of God. But the painting could also be suggesting that anywhere, round any corner, the worship of God is being ignored. Under the leaning roof of the stable there is colour and harmony, but outside it there is a bleak grey, as though only here are life, warmth and reality to be found. Yet the angels are not calling everyone to the manger, filling the whole night sky with light and calling humanity to witness the birth of the Christ child. The music is perfectly audible to the little group caught up in praise, but it can also be easily ignored. People are not flocking out of the town in the background at the sound of the angels' song; here there is only a small group of humans and animals witnessing the full glory of God, listening to the worship of heaven. This will be characteristic of everything God does in Jesus Christ, which means that it is also characteristic of God's whole being, since Jesus is the 'image of the invisible God' (Colossians 1.15).

Everyone who encounters Jesus, throughout his earthly ministry, stands in the presence of the Son of God, whom angels praise endlessly. Jesus' offer of salvation is open to them all, yet some notice and some do not. Even the resurrection, that great triumph of God over death and hell, is witnessed by only a few.

In Advent, we are studying God's strange ways, so very different from our own. God does not come to claim his kingdom with imperial might, overwhelming the opposition; he comes in vulnerability, unobtrusively, changing the world in ways we cannot imagine. The angels spend Advent saying 'Don't be afraid', just as they do to the shepherds. It is not their own terrifying presence they are reassuring us about, but the breathtakingly daring action of God. 'Do not be afraid,' say the Advent angels. 'God knows what needs to be done. Come to the manger.'

To spend Advent in the company of the messengers of God is to become sensitized to the action of God and to the unlikely places in which the worship of the heavens is happening. It may occasionally blaze out, unmistakably, but even then the world will go on its weary way around the singing angels. Those who hear their singing need to take heart, hold on to their courage, and remember that the worship of heaven is endless, indefatigable, never suppressed.

For reflection or discussion

Do you trust that God's ways are the best, or do you wish that God would overwhelm the world with power?

What practices might help make us more sensitive to the places where the worship of heaven is happening?

Lord, open our eyes and hearts to the worship of heaven, taking place all around us, seen and unseen. In the power of the Spirit, help us lift our voices, too, and join the angelic chorus, as we tell the world, 'Fear not.' Amen.

14

Watching
and
waiting: the
visitation

The Visitation,
1491, Domenico
Ghirlandaio

The Gospels are not novels; they are spare in their narrative details, seldom telling us what anyone is thinking or feeling. The gospel writers aim to tell us enough of what they have seen or heard reported so that we, like those who first met Jesus, can make up our own minds about the challenge and opportunity he offers.

Mark's Gospel does not tell us anything at all about Jesus' birth and childhood, while John's Gospel starts with the birth narrative of the cosmos, which comes into existence through the one we are about to encounter in Jesus. Only Matthew and Luke give us our Christmas stories, which we tend to amalgamate into one, without noticing their different emphases. Matthew tells us the story largely from Joseph's point of view, as Joseph accepts the pregnancy he did not cause and protects the son who is not his. It is Luke who gives us Mary's story, though even here there is much left out.

What is striking about Luke's account is that it is all about faithful women. Mary's response to the angelic messenger is contrasted with Zechariah's – Zechariah doubts; Mary accepts. Immediately after the angel's visit, Mary sets off to visit her relative Elizabeth (Luke 1.39). This is where a novelist would go into detail about the emotions of these two women, both miraculously pregnant with sons whose destinies are terrifyingly huge. But all Luke gives us is the moving detail that Elizabeth's unborn child 'leapt for joy' (Luke 1.44) in the presence of Mary's.

It is left to painters to fill out some of the detail of this touching encounter. Ghirlandaio shows us the older woman, Elizabeth,

kneeling to Mary, showing the joy and reverence with which her leaping child is dancing inside her. Yet Elizabeth is a respectable married woman; her husband comes from a well-known priestly family, and although her pregnancy is unexpected and perhaps a little embarrassing at her age, all her friends and neighbours can share in the couple's delight that at last, after so many years of marriage, they are to have a child. Ghirlandaio shows Elizabeth wearing a beautiful, buttercup-yellow robe, as though spring has come to her at last. Mary, on the other hand, is a young unmarried mother, dependent on the goodwill of her fiancé to save her name and enable her to bring up the child in safety. This moment that we are witnessing must have been balm to Mary's storm-tossed soul. Here is someone who understands and believes what has happened to her. Any ignorant onlooker would expect the younger woman to be curtseying to the older, but Elizabeth is demonstrating that the world's order is changing with the birth of Mary's child. Here, in this peaceful little alcove, with the noises of the city far away in the background, these two women support each other as they look to God's new future.

Elizabeth plays no further part in the story, as the Gospels tell it. In view of her age, she may not have lived to see her son, John the Baptist, executed. Mary, on the other hand, will live through her son's ministry, his death and his resurrection, and will be present when the Holy Spirit comes to start the proclamation of her Son as the good news of God's reign (Acts 1—2). The brooch she is wearing in this picture, with its great, blood-red ruby, is a symbol of the pain she will undergo. But, just for this moment, Mary and Elizabeth can comfort each other and rejoice.

Ghirlandaio shows us the intimacy of this moment, as Mary bends down to lift up her cousin. We can feel the strength that these two women are drawing from each other. The painting also hints at the challenge to the world's values, as Mary is about to sing her great Magnificat to God's subversive action. The city, with its man-made buildings and laws, is at a distance, as the picture zooms in on a different system of values. 'He has brought down the powerful,' Mary sings (Luke 1.52), and her and Elizabeth's pregnancies are witness to the irresistible force of God. God does not need an army to overthrow tyrants, because God can bring life where there was none. These pregnancies are part of the same action that will raise Jesus from the dead: they are part of the irrepressible vitality of God.

In Advent, Mary and Elizabeth greet each other and invite us to take comfort in their hope and their witness to God, the life-giver, who has come to be with the humble and meek.

For reflection or discussion

Who are the people to whom you turn when you need comfort or are in doubt?

Are there things that older people could helpfully do to support younger people in their journey of faith?

Lord of power, as you bless the poor and meek, and comfort those who weep and mourn, give us the Spirit to lead us into your ways of compassion and love, through making us disciples of your Son, our saviour, Jesus Christ. Amen.

15

Watching and waiting: the animals

The Noah's Ark on Mount Ararat, 1570, Simon de Myle

Despite all the crib scenes and the Christmas cards, there are no animals mentioned officially in the nativity story. Luke's Gospel says that the newborn baby was laid in a manger, because the town was crowded and there were no free bedrooms in the inn. It is perhaps a natural assumption that where there is a manger for animal feed, there may well be animals, but they are not described. Similarly, Luke tells us that shepherds followed angelic instructions and came to see the newborn baby, but whether they brought any of their sheep with them is not recorded.

But there are good theological grounds for suggesting that it is not only human beings who wait in Advent for the coming of God's salvation. Genesis 1 shows the intricate interdependence of the 'days' of creation, with each emerging from the possibilities set up by the one before, and each, in itself, 'very good'. Genesis 2 describes the newly created human creature naming the animals God brings forth. A name is not just incidental: it speaks of the essence of what is named, so the human being is doing something profoundly formative in naming the nature and destiny of the animals. And in 'tilling and keeping' the garden in which they all live together, the human being is also shaping the environment that all the living creatures God has created will inhabit (Genesis 2.15).

Simon de Myle's painting of Noah's ark on Mount Ararat shows another example of the inextricable connection between the natural world and human action. At God's command, Noah has

conserved enough of the original creation to start again after
the catastrophic floods that have wiped away the rest of the
world. The created order is both devastated and redeemed by
humans – the floods are God's punishment, Genesis says, for the
wickedness of humanity, but Noah, the one righteous person,
saves more than just himself.

John's Gospel says that 'all things' come into being through
the creative power of the Son of God, and although the
Gospels concentrate on the human reaction to Jesus, there are
indications that the created world reacts too. Jesus stills the
storm, walks on water, removes sickness, rides a donkey; in
other words, he interacts with the physical environment as a
human being who is fulfilling the role given to human beings
in that first Genesis theology – to exercise God's power for the
good of all creation. In Romans 8, Paul writes that the whole
of creation is in bondage and, like us, full of hope (Romans
8.21–22). Creation, too, is waiting for God's liberation in Jesus
Christ, just as much as we are, and the two liberations are
inseparable.

De Myle's painting is full of life and detail. We can almost smell
the good fresh air, feel the shaky humans and animals finding
their feet again, after all that time cooped up in the fetid,
swaying depths of the ark. The painting is showing us what
liberation looks like, as all the creatures head off to eat, to
explore, to start their lives again. The ark may have been the
means to this, but it was not the end.

It is tempting to think of 'salvation' as something personal and
individual; this is not wrong, but it is not enough. In Advent,
we are drawn to see that the creator of the world is prepared to

come and live in what is created in order to fill it again with the life that brought it into being in the first place. And that means that salvation is not an offer to us to get into the ark, pull up the drawbridge and stay safe while the rest of the world perishes. Rather, it is an invitation to go out and reclaim the new creation, emerging from the floods.

In the Western world, Advent falls in winter, when the whole world seems to be waiting, full of secret life that cannot yet be seen but can be trusted and longed for. But the cycle of planting and growth is the same whatever the climate, and it is this everyday miracle that Paul uses as a metaphor for the resurrection life in Jesus (1 Corinthians 15). Life and renewal are as much the way of the world as is death: we just need to pay attention to them, in all their glory.

For reflection or discussion

What does 'salvation' mean to you?

Do we tend to think that Jesus comes to get us safely into the ark, or to send us out?

Lord, give us patience and courage to watch and wait, and see the seeds of new life. Send us the Holy Spirit, to bring us to Jesus Christ, the source of life and hope for all the world. Amen.

16

Watching and waiting: Adam and Eve

Expulsion of Adam and Eve from the Garden of Eden, c.1425, Masaccio

Matthew's Gospel starts its preparation for the birth of Jesus with a family tree. This is to make two related but distinct claims about Jesus: the first is that Jesus is to be the successor to David, Israel's greatest king. Under David, the kingdom was united and prosperous, and it knew its proper relationship to God. The loving promises made between God and David are the source of hope for God's people in the time of Jesus, when the land is under Roman rule: God will not abandon his people for ever. Jesus, the Messiah, is the inheritor of those promises, and, with the birth of Jesus, God is coming to set the people free.

But Matthew goes a step further by taking Jesus' family tree even further back in time, to Abraham. Abraham is not a king, but he is the archetype of all faithful response to God. Abraham believes God's promise and is rewarded with a son, born when Abraham and his wife Sarah have given up all hope of children. God promises that this child, Isaac, will be only the beginning of the descendants of Abraham, spreading out to reclaim the earth. God's call to Abraham comes first in Genesis 12, after the painful description of the deterioration of creation from its original glory. God says to Abraham: 'In you all the families of the earth shall be blessed' (Genesis 12.3). In Abraham and his descendants, God is renewing the original blessing to humankind. It is this that Matthew signals by taking Jesus' genealogy back to Abraham: what is about to happen in Jesus is certainly for God's own people, but it is also, through them, for all the peoples of the earth.

Matthew's genealogy also has some intriguing anomalies: very unusually, on several occasions he mentions not just the paternal line but also the maternal descent, and in each case the latter is somewhat irregular. For example, he points out that one of David's ancestresses was the foreigner Ruth (Matthew 1.5), and that Solomon's mother was an adulteress (Matthew 1.6). So the ground has been well prepared for us by the time Matthew gets to Mary in verse 16. God's active blessing constantly occurs in unconventional ways.

Luke's Gospel has a genealogy, too, which traces Jesus' line back to Adam (Luke 3.38) and then to God, since Adam has no other 'father' but the direct action of God. Luke, too, claims that Jesus is the fulfilment of God's original purposes, to bless human beings and to establish a close and loving connection with them.

This genealogical exercise can induce a mood of sad looking back during Advent. It can suggest that the coming of Jesus is primarily about regaining something that has been lost. Masaccio's painting of Adam and Eve being expelled from Eden is powerfully full of shame, remorse, grief and longing: Adam and Eve, weeping bitterly, are overcome with the desire to turn back time. Adam cannot bear to look forward, covering his eyes rather than see what he has lost or where he must go now. Eve's face is a tragic mask, and she tries to cover herself, as though she loathes what she has become. They hardly need the red, wrathful angel with the drawn sword to keep them out – they know what they deserve, what they have brought upon themselves.

But Matthew and Luke are not urging a mood of self-flagellation for Advent. Their genealogies are reminding us of the action of God that is always prior to ours and always creative. God brought all things into being in the first place; God comes, over and over again, to human beings who, like Abraham, like David, are sometimes faithful but often not. God keeps promises when they look impossible, as with the birth of Isaac, and God is not derailed by human unfaithfulness; nothing can stop God from blessing creation. Human beings go on hoping or fearing that they are the sole actors in the universe, and so they constantly forget the irrepressible action of God.

In Advent, we are preparing to meet again the God who cannot be prevented from blessing creation and who cannot be forced to be distant and unloving. God has manifested that character, endlessly, in the history that Matthew and Luke remind us of, and now, in Jesus, this is the God who is coming to live in and with creation, connecting it intimately and undeniably to the divine life again, for ever.

For reflection or discussion

Are you tempted to look back to when things seemed simpler?

Is nostalgia ever a constructive emotion?

Lord, we come to you in penitence for all the ways in which we have damaged ourselves and others; give us the Holy Spirit, we pray, to lead us in trust to your saving work in Jesus Christ, always greater than our sin, and never defeated by our failure. Amen.

17

Watching
and waiting:
the midwife

Birth of Christ,
c.1400, Master of
Salzburg

The accounts that we now have of the ministry, death and
resurrection of Jesus are a form of literature that the gospel
writers seem to have invented, more or less. They bear a strong
resemblance to ancient biographies, but their purpose is not
just to give an account, or even to uphold a reputation, but to
convert. The four Gospels with which we are most familiar are
the ones that gradually gained acceptance through their usage
across the whole Church. In the first few centuries, the good
news of Jesus spread surprisingly effectively across the Roman
Empire, but the Church had no legal or executive power and was
subject to regular persecution, sometimes sporadic and localized,
sometimes more orchestrated and widespread. It was not until
the conversion of the Emperor Constantine in the fourth century
that Christianity had any kind of official backing, which allowed
it to begin to codify and organize. By this point, it was clear that
the Gospels that we call Matthew, Mark, Luke and John were in
widespread use in the dispersed churches, and they came to be
considered 'canonical' – meaning that they were the standard
against which other accounts were to be measured.

There certainly were other 'Gospels', some of which survive
as testimony to the restraint of the canonical Gospels. It is in
one of these other Gospels that we come across the midwife
who attended the birth of Jesus. She is not mentioned by Luke,
who writes about the birth in Bethlehem and the baby laid in a
manger, and about the shepherds summoned by the angels. But
it would not be at all unlikely that one or two local women with
expertise in childbirth came out to help the young woman give

birth to her first child. The artist here shows us two young and wholesome-looking girls, reverently taking the well-developed child from his elegantly attired mother in order to give him his first bath, while Joseph looks on, bored and sleepy. There is no hint of the pain and blood of childbirth, or the dirt and disorder that must have been part of this particular birth, if it really did take place unexpectedly and outside, as Luke suggests.

Although the account that refers to the midwife is considerably later than our canonical gospels, and not particularly edifying – the midwife's arm is withered because she has the temerity to doubt the perpetual virginity of Mary – what is striking is its testimony to the way in which stories of Jesus continued to circulate. It also suggests that our Christian forebears were not endlessly credulous – they could tell the difference between a likely story and an unlikely one.

Stories about Jesus started to circulate almost immediately. It could hardly be otherwise, since his earliest followers began to call others to believe and trust in Jesus. Within a few years of Jesus' death and resurrection, St Paul is already able to cite set traditions about Jesus that are told to all new believers – for example, about the witnesses to the resurrection, and the practice of the shared meal, so characteristic of Christians (see 1 Corinthians 15 and 11).

Luke does not claim to be an eyewitness, but he tells us at the beginning of the Gospel and in Acts that he went around collecting evidence and doing research, presumably at a time when there were still plenty of people about who had met Jesus, travelled with him, witnessed his teaching, his miracles, his death and his resurrection. Centuries later, despite the terrible destruction of the war that raged through the territory, Christians were able to point out the locations of many of the events narrated in the Gospels when Constantine began to search for the holy places and build sites of worship in the key areas.

Yet there must also have been so many stories that were not widely told, though perhaps treasured locally. Perhaps the neighbours who had been among the 5,000 whom Jesus fed got together from time to time and reminisced, or the lepers who had been healed reminded their friends and relations about how their lives had been changed.

Testimony – telling the story of what Jesus has done – is a vital part of Christian faith. An encounter with Jesus is converting, but never just for one person: it is to be shared, as a witness to the action of God. If there were indeed midwives present at the birth of Jesus, what a tale they had to tell.

For reflection or discussion

What is your testimony to what God has done in your life?

Why do we find it difficult to share our testimonies?

Lord, give us thankful hearts and renew in us the gift of the Holy Spirit, to make us ready to tell the good news of what you have done in our lives, through Jesus Christ, our Lord. Amen.

18

Watching and waiting: the Roman Empire

The Roman Empire did not realize that it was helping to prepare for Christmas, yet in Luke's telling of the birth of Jesus, the bean-counting tendencies of the Empire had a significant part to play. The Emperor Augustus's decision to call for a census ensured that Jesus was born in Bethlehem of Judea. Unwittingly, the emperor was helping to fulfil a prophecy.

The Roman Empire was one of the most long-lasting and successful of imperial experiments. At the time of Jesus, it held territory all around the Mediterranean basin, and its educated citizens shared a culture and a sense of belonging: it was possible for Paul to invoke his Roman citizenship as a protection in the first century, although he was a Jew from Tarsus, and for Augustine to get a high-ranking university post in Milan in the fourth century, although he was a small-town boy from North Africa.

Tiepolo shows us the mighty Augustus, among the most long-lived and successful of Roman emperors. Inscriptions to his successes hailed him as divine and as a saviour. Here, he sits enthroned, never doubting his power to judge, wielding life and death.

So Luke's point is subtle and subversive. The great might of the Roman Empire is put to use by God for quite different purposes. The angelic host do not arrive to sing at the birth of Caesar but for the birth of Jesus. Empires come and go, but God is eternal, and God's plans were in place long before the Roman Empire came into being, and they remain.

The Gospels all speak of the work of Jesus as claiming a 'kingdom' for God. Although Jesus goes about this in unusual ways, the fact remains that his claim is as much political as it is spiritual. Jesus does not take his mission to the top, ingratiating himself with rulers and leaders; instead, he heals, teaches, forgives and feeds the ordinary people. His ministry says something vital about the nature of true kingship and throws down a challenge to all other kinds of power. Power is given so that the powerless can be protected and cared for, and yet that is so seldom the use that is made of it. No wonder the powerful found Jesus an unbearable irritant, with his lack of concern for his own safety, wealth and status, and yet with all that power at his disposal.

The Gospels show the increasingly raw confrontations between Jesus and those who hold power, whether religious or civic. In both spheres, Jesus exercises the power of God to attend to the needy, rather than put systems in place to protect the status quo. In Advent, we watch and wait as God prepares the new kingdom, the kingdom of God. Mary sings of the strength of God, which is used to scatter the proud and fill the hungry (Luke 1.51–53); Zechariah sings to his unborn son, John, who will prepare the way for the mighty saviour, who will bring in the time of forgiveness, salvation, tender mercy and light in darkness (Luke 1.76–79). They both speak of the overwhelming power of God, compared with which empires crumble.

Throughout Advent, we are relearning the nature of kingship and the nature of the kingdom to which we are called. What we see at work in the birth of Jesus is the immense power of God. God the creator of all things, who exists before time, outside time, whose very being is life, has the power to live a temporal life, and even to die. This ought not to be possible. It is wholly contradictory, making a nonsense of all our definitions of God. But God defines God, and apparently God sees no contradiction: this is how the power of God was, is and always will be – the power of life and love, always.

Augustus lived longer than many Roman emperors and had a significant effect on history, but he is dead and gone. The Roman Empire was among the most extensive and successful outworkings of human power, but it passed. Only Jesus, the child whose birth we are preparing for, is raised from the dead and sits at the right hand of the Father, as ruler and judge for ever. So only Jesus' way of wielding power can ultimately conquer, because it will not be superseded. We are preparing to learn to trust and exercise that kind of power.

For reflection or discussion

Are you aware that you sometimes exercise power in un-Christlike ways?

How might Christians critique how we use power?

Mighty Lord, we pray that you will free us from the enchantments of the power that cannot give life, and lead us in the ways of your kingdom, as the Holy Spirit pours out your power in lives transformed into the likeness of Jesus Christ, your Son. Amen.

19

O Wisdom

Holy Wisdom, 1670s

In the last few days before Christmas, the custom is to praise the child who is about to be born, highlighting aspects of his character as they have been known throughout the ages. The child of Bethlehem is not a new God, but the one, true God, our creator, who has been calling human beings from the moment we were made. What we see in Jesus is the fullness of the character of God.

This icon praises the wisdom of God, through which creation came into existence, and which is found, personified, in Jesus. It is unusual to find a depiction of it, but the title is one that is often ascribed to Jesus. When the earliest Christians were searching back through Scripture for references to Jesus, the figure of Wisdom in Proverbs 8 and in the Wisdom of Solomon 7 resonated. Proverbs 8 describes Wisdom's role with God in creation, and the joy that they share; Wisdom is God's 'darling and delight', 'playing over his whole world' (Proverbs 8.30–31, REB), and the Wisdom of Solomon says that Wisdom is 'the flawless mirror of the active power of God, and the image of his goodness' (Wisdom 7.26, NEB). The similarity to the Christian understanding of the relationship between Father and Son made these obvious texts to go to.

In the icon, the figure of Jesus stands just above Wisdom, claiming and affirming her as an insight into his own character. Mary and John the Baptist stand either side of Wisdom, and also attest to her as the likeness of Jesus, with all the authority of the mother and the forerunner. Wisdom sits on the seven pillars on

which the universe is founded; she is dressed in vivid colours, making herself available to us, full of energy and passion. There is nothing insipid about Wisdom: she is forceful and attractive. The attention and praise that are given to her are channelled upwards to the figure of Christ, and from him still further up to the Father's throne, where the angels echo earth's praise.

There is no embarrassment at all about the identification of the feminine Wisdom with Jesus – that seems to be a relatively modern preoccupation. Augustine talks easily about the 'breasts of the Father' from which we are fed; Julian of Norwich describes Jesus as a mother pelican, tearing her own breast to feed her children; Jesus describes himself as a mother hen; Hosea pictures God as a mother helping her infant with its first toddling, unsteady steps. The images that best help us to catch glimpses of the character of God are used without gender distinction.

In Advent, we are encouraged to meditate on the wisdom of God, recognizing that it is both deeply engrained in the universe and yet also alien and elusive. It is God's wisdom that is coming to birth in a baby who has no power and no status, who will live a short, unsuccessful life and die a painful and shameful death. This is the wisdom of God at work. We trace its contours in the life of Jesus: the little boy who understands the Scriptures better than the experts in the Temple; the young man who unerringly calls a motley crew of disciples to him, entrusting them with the good news for the world; the teacher who sees into the heart of the rich young ruler, of Zacchaeus, of the woman at the well; the fierce opponent, who challenges all those who try to keep God boxed in; the strategist, who avoids capture and death until the perfect moment. This is wisdom embodied. It can be misunderstood, ignored, rejected, but it cannot be defeated, as the resurrection shows. It is the reality of the universe.

Learning to live in the wisdom of God is learning to attend to and trust what God has made. There is no conflict between 'knowledge' and 'wisdom': both are about what is true, and how to honour it and live in tune with it. The early Christians called Jesus both 'wisdom' and 'word', Sophia and Logos. The universe is rational; it is meant to be open to our exploration and delight, and we flourish when we live by its rhythms and needs. The universe, like us, takes its character from the one through whom it came into existence. At its heart, there is delight, joy, generous communication. Now, in Advent, we respond with praise and find ourselves living in wisdom. God is coming to invite us to play in the presence of the Son, for the joy of all that is made.

For reflection or discussion

Do you believe yourself to be a source of joy to God?

Why do you think we have become uncomfortable with feminine descriptions of God?

Come, Holy Spirit, and lead us in the ways of wisdom, that we may live with you and the Lord Jesus Christ, delighting in the presence of the Father. Amen.

20
O Adonai

Landscape with Moses and the Burning Bush, 1616, Domenichino

Adonai is another of the great Advent declarations of the nature of God. It is a title given to God in Jewish devotion, often to avoid saying the divine name, which is too holy and powerful for any human being to utter safely. Adonai is also the title given to God when we humans admit the divine Lordship – God is the Lord, and we are God's servants.

This is an aspect of God's character that is easy to underemphasize, particularly at this time of year. We look at the birth of the tiny, vulnerable baby; we think of the myrrh, foreshadowing his coming death, and we rightly marvel at the willingness of God to become truly human. In the midst of this, it is easy to overlook the fact that God becomes human in order to reclaim the world. There is an interplay between God's power and God's humility that is hard for us to take in, because we do not see the two as interconnected in the way that God apparently does.

Domenichino paints an encounter that vividly brings out these aspects of our relationship with God, who is both Lord and servant. Exodus 3 says that Moses was keeping his father-in-law's sheep, having run away from Egypt after killing an Egyptian bully. Suddenly, Moses see the most peculiar sight – a bush that is burning without disintegrating. There is a tiny hint in the text that God has been trying to attract Moses' attention for a while by the time that Moses finally goes to examine the bush: 'when the Lord saw that he had turned aside to see' (Exodus 3.4).

The painting shows the moment when God speaks to Moses out of the bush. Moses is on his knees, shielding his face from the impossible glory blazing out of the bush. His bare feet acknowledge that he is in a holy place, like a temple, and he is clinging on to his staff for dear life, as the one familiar thing in this unprecedented situation. The sheep seem far less bothered – but then the Lord is not addressing them.

Yet after this display of sheer power, which Moses cannot deny, there follows an almost comic dialogue between God and Moses. Faced with the holy and terrible blaze, Moses still argues with God. God is calling Moses to return to Egypt and free the people of Israel, to confront the pharaoh and demand the release of his slaves. Not surprisingly, Moses does not want to do it, but it *is* surprising that he has the temerity to argue when faced with God's power. There must be something in the way in which God draws Moses into dialogue that allows Moses to feel, even in the face of this overwhelming display of power, that he is still valued, his co-operation requested, not coerced. God is not enslaving Moses in order to free others. Freedom is God's goal, and that means Moses' freedom, as well as that of the children of Israel.

God goes to extraordinary lengths to encourage Moses that he is capable of what God is asking. God reveals to Moses the mysterious name by which people may know that this is indeed their God; God shows Moses the miraculous powers that will be at his disposal. Finally, in Exodus 4, Moses pleads personal inability, but he is beginning to capitulate. In 4.10, Moses acknowledges that God is 'my Lord', with the implication that Moses must therefore serve. He lasts out a bit longer, arguing and wriggling, but he has hit the truth – God is his Lord.

Domenichino has made no attempt to paint this encounter as a historical event. This is not a desert region somewhere in the Middle East, but his own native country. There in the background is a beautiful Italian lake, with a little castle perched idyllically on a small hill, surrounded by lush grass. This happens to be Moses' encounter with the divine power, but it is happening in Domenichino's time and country. This happens to be God's call to Moses to fulfil his particular vocation, but, by implication, the burning bush awaits any of us: we might come upon our encounter with God and God's call on our lives anywhere. Domenichino is urging us to attend, so that we will notice our burning bush and leave our accustomed path to investigate and so find out who we are. Moses could have denied God's right to be Lord over his life, but then he would never have discovered the story of Moses, told for centuries and millennia, the story of the man who was God's servant, and so was able to set the people free.

For reflection or discussion

Do you think you sometimes focus on personal weaknesses as an excuse not to do and be what God is calling you to?

Why do you think God does not just make Moses obey?

Come, Holy Spirit, and show us in Jesus' life of self-giving service that to serve the Father is blessing, honour, freedom and hope. Amen.

21

O Root of Jesse

The Tree of Jesse

This lovely icon shows Jesus at the heart of the family tree of the house of David. On each branch sits one of the heroes of Israel, gazing at Jesus, who is at the centre of the tree, pointing to the Scriptures that witness to him. This is what the whole story has been about.

This Advent proclamation of the character of Jesus comes from one of Isaiah's most lyrical descriptions of the world put right by God. In Isaiah 11, the prophet speaks of the 'shoot' that will come from the 'stump of Jesse'. The tree that looks dead, looks as though its story is at an end, will blossom again, and with it the new age will dawn. Isaiah describes the coming one as wise, strong and just. Nothing deceives God's Messiah, because he does not judge by human standards but by divine, and so the world can at last be at peace. 'The wolf shall live with the lamb, the leopard shall lie down with the kid, the calf and the lion and the fatling together, and a little child shall lead them' (Isaiah 11.6–7). The icon evokes the mood of joyful peace, with its lovely symmetry and the haloing circle of leaves against the vivid, royal gold background. Jesus, the judge, sits comfortably at the heart of the curves and lines of the painting, drawing it together, giving it focus. This is the judgement that Isaiah is talking about, where everything finds its proper meaning and symmetry. This judgement is not primarily terrifying, but restorative: at last, the lovely truth of the universe is visible.

Paul uses this image of the 'root of Jesse' in Romans 15. Although this may look like someone else's family tree, with no room for the rest of us, Paul picks up what Isaiah, too, affirms. This story of the

house of David is a story for the whole world. 'The nations shall inquire of' this root of Jesse, Isaiah says (Isaiah 11.10), and Paul says that 'in him the Gentiles shall hope' (Romans 15.12). The icon shows Jesus not as one of the branches of the tree, but as the continuation of the trunk, and the Advent acclamation calls Jesus 'the root' of the tree; he is not just its product but also its source.

One of the resurrection stories that Luke gives us is of a couple walking in deep dejection on the road to Emmaus, mourning the death of Jesus and of all their hopes in him. They meet a stranger, who takes them back through Scripture to show them that God has not made a mistake in what has happened to Jesus. Throughout the gospels, Jesus draws people back to Scripture, asking them to hear it and interpret it more carefully. He displays the kind of familiarity and mastery of Scripture that the icon helps us to see. Here is Jesus, the word of God, helping us to re-read the words of Scripture in his light.

Although the icon is peaceful and speaks of completion, it expects us to pick up on the symbolism of the tree. This is the tree that represents that tree in the garden of Eden, whose fruit Adam and Eve chose in preference to their obedience to God; each branch holds a part of the story of human selfishness and disobedience that leads to the tree of the cross on which Jesus dies. The prophecies of Isaiah speak of the suffering servant, as well as of the wise and invincible judge. God will hold the two together in the great act of salvation. As we trace this 'family tree', it is an exploration of the faithfulness of God, through all things. God created the world to hold it close in love and vitality, and whatever we choose, we cannot make God change. This is the nature of God, as Jesus shows us, pointing to the Scripture.

It is easy to read this family tree – any family tree – whether with pride or pain, as something that shapes us, explains us, and that is true, up to a point. But what it can easily leave out is the action of God. The tree of Jesse is the tree from which all life springs, and it has its source and its fulfilment in God. Any and every family tree can bear unexpected fruit, even when it seems defunct or deadly, because its life comes from the life of God.

For reflection or discussion

Is your family tree a source of pride or fear to you?

How can we learn to read Scripture more faithfully?

Come, Holy Spirit, and open the Scriptures to us, so that our story may find its truth in Jesus Christ, the Son who draws all families home to the Father. Amen.

22
O Key of David

David and Goliath,
c.1857, Edgar Degas

David is one of the most vivid and likeable of the wide range of characters in the Old Testament. He is brave, talented, passionate and flawed. He loves absolutely, though not always wisely. He comes at a turning point and pinnacle in Israel's history, and has almost the weight of the garden of Eden in evoking nostalgia. In the reign of David, there was an unbreakable bond between God and the king, and so the people could feel assured of their position at the heart of God's action. It is not surprising that David looms large in Advent, as a human figure who carries God's message of love and hope.

David is Israel's second king, and the one chosen directly by God. After years of being led by prophets and 'judges', the people notice that most of the neighbouring countries have kings, and they decide they want one too. Saul is chosen by lot, but also because he looks the part – he is head and shoulders taller than all the men around him. But Saul turns out to have few other kingly attributes, and God sends Samuel the prophet to anoint another king, one of Jesse's sons, from Bethlehem. As in any good story, David is the youngest brother, the one most likely to be overlooked, off in the fields, looking after the sheep when Samuel arrives to look for God's chosen king (1 Samuel 16).

Degas sketches David the shepherd boy, armed only with his sling, facing the gigantic Philistine champion, Goliath. Degas has not chosen to show the contrast between the small, unarmed boy and the huge, breast-plated soldier. Instead, because David is in the foreground, Goliath looks almost negligible. We are seeing

David's spirit and courage, his arm confidently poised to whirl the fatal stone, his hair ruffled in the breeze. Inside David's head, Goliath is already defeated.

It is perhaps this bold willingness to be vulnerable and to use overlooked and unlikely strength that is David's 'key'. In Isaiah 22.22, God speaks through the prophet, saying that a day will come when a faithful steward will wield 'the key of the house of David' with such authority that he will be able to hold any door, either closed to the enemy or open to a friend. Revelation 3.7–8 puts that key in the hand of Jesus. 'I know you have but little power,' Jesus says to the church in Philadelphia, but if Jesus is the keyholder, then no enemy, however apparently mighty, can prevail against them.

David does not try to use Goliath's weapons. He is not overawed into believing that there is only one kind of strength. He brings what he is to the fight: he is a shepherd boy; he has spent years defending his sheep from wild animals, never needing a sword or armour, and he does not lose confidence now, just because Goliath has more conventional weaponry. Psalm 78.70 says that God chose David precisely because of his shepherding skills. David brings to his kingly task the heart that was formed by caring for the defenceless sheep. The psalm pictures David 'nursing ewes', sheep at their most vulnerable, having just lambed. That is what God was looking for in a king.

When we acclaim Jesus as the 'key of David', this is the cluster of characteristics we are calling to mind. Jesus is willing to be vulnerable, and to use skills and gifts that do not look like those of a conquering king; but, like David, Jesus is also to be trusted to notice and care for the needy. That is why we rejoice in the

fact that Jesus is the one with the key: he will open the door
for us because we are poor, needy, defenceless and foolish. This
is not a door we can open by ourselves, with our own strength
or wisdom, but that is not a problem, because the shepherd
king holds the door. Our Advent challenge is to trust that this
is indeed the case. We look at David, a boy with a sling; we look
at Jesus, a man with the marks of the nails in his hands and his
feet, and our instinct is to turn to Goliath, who has the armour
and looks like a champion.

Degas' sketch shows us the sheer exuberance and exhilaration
of David's trust in the unlikely weapon whirling above his head.
This is the beginning of an adventure to discover what kind of
might a shepherd has.

For reflection or discussion

What is your 'slingshot' – the thing about you that God is waiting
to use?

Are there situations in which we need to be willing to be
vulnerable, and not to use the tactics that everyone else uses?

Come, Holy Spirit, and lead us to the door which Jesus alone can
hold open, and which leads to the Father's home. Amen.

23

O Morning Star

The Harrowing of Hell, fourteenth century

Those of us who live in brightly lit towns and cities may not know what it is to wait with longing for the morning star, visible when all around is still dark, heralding the approach of daylight. Where there is no artificial light, the morning star brings a slight but marked alteration in the quality of the surrounding darkness. It hovers tantalizingly on the edge of dark and daylight. It is perhaps this liminal quality that makes it a powerful Advent title for Jesus: as we wait for this birth that heralds God's conquest of the dark, we are still in a contested world, one where the darkness still seems in control, and yet there is the glimmer of light as the one star emerges.

In the Bible, light and dark are often motifs that circle around choice and judgement. In Romans 13.12, salvation is the bright day we are longing for, just over the horizon, and now is the time of the morning star; soon it will be broad daylight, and we must be ready for all our deeds to be seen. There is a mixture of hope and fear in these motifs, as we both long for and shrink from the life-giving, revelatory light. We cannot live without it, but somehow we have persuaded ourselves that our grey half-lit lives are enough.

The coming of the day is inexorable: nothing can hold it back, no one can delay it, and yet it comes so gently that it is hard to say at which precise moment the day starts and the night is definitely over. Like so many of the Advent themes, this calls us to reimagine the power of God at work in Jesus.

The Harrowing of Hell from Jerez de la Frontera shows us the contrast between different kinds of power. In the background, filling the top of the picture, is the huge hell-monster, full of teeth and flames, with enraged, inflamed eyes. Its dark minions, shooting flame from their mouths, try to terrify the timid human beings, moving wonderingly towards the light. The men and women are packed together, hardly able to move, naked and defenceless, and yet their eyes are alight with hope, and each one has the beginning of a small smile. They had thought daylight was gone for ever and yet, suddenly, the great jaws have opened, and there is nothing to prevent them simply stepping out.

Their rescuer, Jesus, has no visible weapons. He is barefoot, with the marks of the nails still visible. He carries nothing but a slender staff of light, and yet he cannot be stopped. Adam has taken the outstretched, wounded hand confidently, climbing out of the jaws of death; beside him, Eve looks more anxious, still clutching her apple. It is almost as though she half-doubts whether she deserves this. But her progeny are pressing forward, and soon she will step into the light, ransomed, healed, restored, forgiven.

As we watch, history is being rewritten. The history of the human race used to be a history of endless failure and despair, leading to death and darkness. Each individual history, like Eve's, used to be a story of what we have done wrong and cannot undo once we realize the cost. But then here is Jesus, treading lightly over the cinders and the serpents, carrying the wounds of all our viciousness and failure, but refusing to accept that they tell the whole story. The story of the world was never ours to ruin and take into endless night; the world belongs to God and, in Jesus Christ, God tells the story over. It is still pitiful and terrible, but now it ends differently.

The child whose birth we are awaiting is, like all children, born to die. But he dies in order to reclaim death and judgement as the province of God; it no longer belongs to the fanged monster of darkness, but to the coming day.

When Eve finally plucks up courage and steps out of the monster's jaws, she gives her apple to Jesus, who takes it, breaks it, and offers it as life for the world. She just has to be brave and humble enough to believe that Jesus has the power to re-make the meaning of the apple. That is no slight thing: all this time, the story of the apple has been one of the terrible power she wielded, and it has made her who she is. Now she must choose if she is willing to be the daughter of the living one, rather than the mother of all those who must die.

For reflection or discussion

What do you think your 'apple' is – the thing that both forms and deforms you?

Do we believe it is really possible for people to change?

Come, Holy Spirit, and lift our eyes to the bright day dawning in Jesus Christ. Give us courage to live as children of the light, for the glory of God the Father. Amen.

24

O King of
the Nations

*Elohim Creating
Adam*, 1795, William
Blake

Blake's depiction of the creation of Adam is by no means a celebration of life. Blake was deeply ambivalent about the theological narrative that seems to say that we are created good but constantly judged for being unable to live up to our origins. It is as though we are blamed for being what we are. This painting is full of pain and bitter symbolism. The winged creator figure, whom Blake called Elohim, rather than God, has a look of fierce, abstracted effort on his face, as he wrenches Adam out of the ground. His left hand is clenching the earth, as though he is having to tear it away from Adam. Adam, too, looks full of terrible sorrow, his left hand desperately reaching back into the watery darkness beneath him, which represents the homely nothingness he longs for, and from which he is being forcibly removed.

Even as the earth begins to recede, the human form is already manacled to its deathly destiny. Already, the serpent is coiled around Adam's leg, which ends in a hoof. He is an unclean thing, bereft of choice, from the start. Adam longs to be uncreated, disembodied, returned to nothingness, rather than burdened with this earthly life in which no freedom from sin is possible.

Blake's tragic vision of human destiny rings true: from this terrible beginning flows a human race constantly forced, almost against its will, to wage war on each other and wreak havoc on the earth. At Advent, we call out to Jesus as the King of the Nations, the one who can take the responsibility of this tragic history from our shoulders, and lift from us the weight of rule and governance that we are so incapable of exercising well.

There is no sense that Blake intended this echo, yet the racked figure of Adam seems to prefigure that of Jesus, laid out on the cross, his arms outstretched, his hands waiting for the impact of the hammered nails. Just as Blake's Adam is made unclean by his creation, as symbolized by his cloven hoof, so too was Jesus' punishment designed to declare him unclean – 'anyone hung on a tree is under God's curse' (Deuteronomy 21.23). Paul picks up the reference in Galatians 3.13, with the extraordinary statement that Christ becomes 'a curse for us'. The bitter, enslaved humanity Blake seems to show us is one that Jesus deliberately takes upon himself. If this is indeed what it is to be human, then this is where Jesus will go.

But Jesus comes to this state as 'King of the Nations'. Adam is not the fount of the human race, the matrix through which its meaning must be read – Jesus is. If we can imagine Blake's picture of creation being mapped on to one of the crucifixion where the human figure is now Jesus, then what we are seeing is what is described in Ephesians 2.15–22; Jesus is making a new humanity. The fragmented pieces of the old humanity are nailed to the cross and put to death, so that what is reborn is the new nation of which Jesus is king. We are no longer 'strangers and aliens', as Blake's Adam is to his hated existence; instead, we are 'members of the household of God'.

Sad, egocentric, embittered and self-obsessed as we are, we have tended to assume that Jesus became human like us, but now, illuminatingly, we discover that we are invited to become human like him. Jesus is the original, in whose likeness we are dreamed. As we wipe away the clinging soil, unwind the grave clothes, what we find is our humanity, rejoicing. Ours is not a fearful legacy, where we are called to be what we cannot be and judged when we fail. Instead, we are invited home, where all our sins are forgiven, nailed to the tree.

The Advent assertion that Jesus is King of the Nations is one that reclaims the creation vision of the oneness of human family, all made from the same dust, all tracing our blood lines back to one progenitor, all given a joint share in the one world. In Jesus, all of this comes together again. Here, again, we find we are one human race, not fragmented by enmity; sharing one world, not fighting to break it into pieces; knowing one source, owing allegiance to one king.

So look again – Adam or Jesus? Life torn from the earth, or life offered to the earth? Desolation or restoration? Expulsion or homecoming?

For reflection or discussion

Do you feel hopeful about your life?

What practical things can we do to live as though we believe that Jesus is 'King of the Nations'?

Come, Holy Spirit, and draw us, rejoicing, into the kingdom where Jesus reigns over all, enthroned at the right hand of the Father. Amen.

25

O Emmanuel

Nativity, 2013,
He Qi

It is such a deceptively simple phrase – God with us, Emmanuel, yet it makes theologies, philosophies, and political theories reel.

He Qi's nativity scene shows both the sweet simplicity and the dazzling complexity of what it is we celebrate at Christmas. At the heart of the picture are the Virgin and Child, in lovely pastel colours, their heads together in the idyllic pose of a mother holding her beloved firstborn. For the moment, Mary is unconscious of the line that slices between her and the baby, the sword that will pierce her heart; for the moment, the apple is just a bright and wholesome toy, but it echoes back to the garden of Eden.

The geometric lines create a sense of turbulence as worlds collide around this birth. Joseph plants his strong foot firmly on the platform where the Mother and Child sit, and holds his lantern up watchfully; he will do all he can to protect his little family from the intersecting currents that swirl around. Some of the lines seem to be creating waves of joy: the sheep, for example, seem to be dancing to a music that only they can hear, while the shepherds are caught up in the turbulence created by the angel. The slats and lines in the background of the picture make it look almost as if this is a windmill rather than a stable, as though the shelter where the family crouch is about to start wheeling and turning around the child, who simply sits in his mother's arms, accepting what is to come.

This one act of God redefines so much. It redefines God. The one who is not an object in the universe but its source and sustainer enters into creation and becomes part of it. God who is the unmoved mover, the only being who exists so absolutely that there is no need to seek a prior cause, God who is, by definition, beyond human knowledge, comes to be God with us, Emmanuel. This act of God redefines power. It takes all the might of the creator of the universe to enter into creation and become the opposite of God. It takes shocking force to absorb hatred and violence and death and turn them into love, peace and life. It lays down a challenge to all other power structures: will they measure up? It is an act of such wild rationality, to show human beings that they both are and are not the centre of the universe. They always thought the universe revolved around them, and they are right – insofar as they are prepared to find themselves redefined in Emmanuel, God with us. The universe revolves around this human being, and those who find themselves in him by giving themselves up, to him and to each other.

He Qi's nativity scene is refracted through a prismatic mirror, warning us of all that is to come. The Roman Empire has its own world to protect, where might is right. Soon, Herod will advance to defend his throne by slaughter. The religious world has its own mirror, which shows the Mother and Child in a dubious light. This is not how God behaves. Soon the teachers and priests will move in and point out how little Emmanuel knows about God's real nature. The shepherds will go home, but others will come, hoping to find health, wealth and happiness, telling Emmanuel what God is for, and losing interest when Emmanuel has other ideas. So many different views of this one act, all of them seeking to make it suit their own purposes.

But, for the moment, the sheep dance, the angel sings, Joseph and the donkey watch the child, and Mary cuddles him. God is given into our hands. God with us.

The angel is singing 'Fear not'. This is still God, even if it is miraculously 'God with us'. God still knows God's business; God still knows how to be God. Nothing that will happen as God lives with us will make God's nature change. God will remain loving, creative, living, renewing through all of life and into death, so that we can be sure that God is with us, always, everywhere, bringing new life, new hope, new possibilities. God with us means that our possibilities, our hopes and fears, are not the limits of what can be. God redefines what is possible, as only God who makes all possibilities can. If God is with us, then so is life and hope. Perhaps the strange lines that intersect across He Qi's nativity scene are the signs of the movement of God, restoring the world.

For reflection or discussion

What places and situations make it hardest to believe that God is with us?

Do you think we have really allowed the Incarnation to define God for us, or are we still bringing an idea of God into our faith from somewhere else?

Come, Holy Spirit, and open our eyes to the wonder of Emmanuel, the Father's gift of Jesus Christ, our saviour and our Lord. Amen.

26
Nativity

The still point of Kershisnik's picture is the three women,
absorbed in the child. They have no eyes for anything around
them. Mary is weary but utterly contented, already the pain
and the blood of childbirth fading as the new life begins to take
on reality. The lovely curve of darkness around her mirrors her
complete lack of interest in anything beyond, as well as her
trust in Joseph and the two young women who have helped
to bring her safely here, to this moment. The midwives, too,
are transfixed by the baby. They must have seen this sight so
often before; perhaps each one is magical, or perhaps there is
something particular about this one. It will not be long before
they notice something going on around them – the hosts of
heaven are already brushing past their heads.

If Mary feels completely secure, leaning back against what looks
like a rucksack, anchored only by Joseph's strength, Joseph's
attitude suggests that he does not feel quite up to the task. He
receives the full force of the gaze of the myriad angels, and he
is not coping well. He has had to deal with so much already,
sticking by Mary through all the months of sniggering and
innuendo. He had expected that the birth of the child would be
the beginning of the next stage of shouldering this God-given
burden, helping Mary to bring up the baby. But it looks as though
he wasn't quite ready for the scale of what he is in for. Joseph
has had dealings with angels before – see Matthew 1.20–23 – but
that was in a dream, and confined safely to the personal and
private realm of his devotion to God. There is nothing private
about this cloud of witnesses, streaming in, pointing and peering,

claiming this birth, this mother and child, as their business. Mary may think she is leaning on Joseph, and that his hand on her shoulder is offering comfort and strength, but Joseph may well be feeling that it is the other way round.

There is a strong sense of momentum in the picture, as the angelic horde blow in from the left and sail off to the right. They do not stay to snuggle up with the baby in warmth and contentment: they are witnesses, messengers, and they have work to do. Soon the whole world will know that Jesus is born. The mother dog, with her litter of puppies, is watching the departing angels with great delight; this is good news for the rest of creation, too. God has come to restore all things from the inside, and all creation 'waits with eager longing' (Romans 8.19).

This event that we are celebrating is both mundane and extraordinary. Babies are born every day, in all kinds of circumstances, and it is nearly always something to be shared, even if only by a very few. Birth is dangerous and painful, and new babies cannot always be assured of a welcome and a place of safety. This is the process to which God incarnate submits himself, avoiding none of the reality, setting up no extra protections. The Son of God is born and becomes the son of Mary and Joseph of Nazareth. This birth honours all births – God does not despise the normal processes of life but enters into them. In the light of this birth, every birth speaks of the coming of God among us in vulnerability, asking our response, not demanding it, inviting us to nurture the growing child, not just to be nurtured by him. This is news about the kind of God we are encountering, and it is news that we need to witness to in our lives and in our world.

Telling the story of Jesus is a life-changing thing to do. If this is the story of God, then this is the story, too, of the true nature of the world. Witnesses of this birth look with new eyes at the hungry and thirsty, at strangers and prisoners, at the naked or the sick (Matthew 25.35), because who knows quite where God might turn up next? This birth helps us to re-train our eyes and hearts so that we get better at focusing, noting, identifying the unlikely ways of God, now that we are coming to know better how God acts. The witnesses in Kershisnik's painting swirl around the Mother and Child, making a protective space for them even as they proclaim the good news. The space and the good news are inseparable; our place of safety is the safety we make for others.

For reflection or discussion

Are there people for whom you can help to make a safe space?

What kind of words and acts that witness to the nature of God can you imagine?

Lord, give us courage to see the birth of your Son, Jesus Christ, as good news for a sad and weary world, and send us out in the power of your Spirit, to witness to what we have seen. Amen.

27
Nativity with the Holy Spirit

Much of Christmas can go by without mentioning the Holy Spirit. Very properly at this time of year, our imaginations tend to focus on the human family, with the occasional thought for the divine Father–Son relationship that is to be made visible in the obedient, loving life of Jesus of Nazareth. But God is Trinity – Father, Son and Holy Spirit – and all of God is involved in everything God does, including the Christmas gift.

This strange picture of the interaction between Mary and the Holy Spirit is an annunciation scene by an artist who has clearly paid attention to the Gospels. Matthew 1.18 says that Mary 'was found to be with child from the Holy Spirit', and in Luke 1.34–35, when Mary asks how the angel's message can be true, since the natural means of pregnancy are not available to her, the angel replies, 'The Holy Spirit will come upon you.' This is the moment that the painter is trying to capture. The expression on Mary's face is hard to read: it is not exactly either fear or acceptance; it looks more like challenge. Certainly, Mary appears to be the powerful one here. The Spirit is small in comparison, vulnerable; Mary's raised hand could bat it away with ease. And that is important: Mary is not a victim in this scene, but a free agent, acting in the power of her own personality and choice. The Holy Spirit enables her to find in herself the strong and adventurous Mary who can bring Jesus to birth, the same Mary who sings the Magnificat – 'My soul magnifies the Lord … all generations will call me blessed.' There is nothing here that diminishes Mary.

There is, of course, a particularity to Mary's encounter with the Holy Spirit: only she gives birth to Jesus and only she is his mother. But the way in which Mary and the Holy Spirit work together reflects something of the continuing work of the Holy Spirit in each one of us. What the Holy Spirit is always doing is bringing Son-shaped, Jesus-shaped lives into being, in a way that releases us to be most truly what we are.

The next time we meet the Holy Spirit in the Gospels is at the baptism of Jesus, when Father and Spirit pour their presence and words of love over the Son: 'You are . . . the Beloved; with you I am well pleased.' In Romans 8.15–16, Paul reminds us that this is the work of the Spirit in every Christian: we learn to say, 'Abba, Father', as Jesus does, and so we learn that we, too, are beloved and bring pleasure to the Father. Paul calls this the Spirit 'bearing witness' to what we are, because we are so timid and uncertain, so prone to doubting that we are indeed adopted into God's family as children, along with Jesus. The Spirit builds up our sense of belonging, making 'son-' and 'daughter-shaped' lives in us.

Perhaps this brings a certain family likeness to Christians, but, as the fresco of the encounter between Mary and the Spirit highlights, the work of the Spirit is not to make clones, but to encourage and celebrate the fullness of each individual: 'varieties of gifts, but the same Spirit', is how Paul describes it (1 Corinthians 12.4). God creates abundance and glories in it; there is nothing small or diminishing in the encounter with God. Mary, the girl from a small backwater of the Roman Empire, steps out on to the pages of history, to be loved, admired, depended upon and held on to as an example for all people at all times.

Of course, Mary's yes was not without cost. Allowing the Holy Spirit to make our lives Jesus-shaped is likely to bring us to the cross, sooner or later, because Jesus-shaped lives are still too challenging for the world to bear: they call into question all the violently self-seeking devices we use to protect ourselves from what we fear. But in Acts 1, there is Mary, in the upper room, among the disciples. She has allowed herself to go on saying yes to the Holy Spirit, and to make her grief and pain a source of life and hope for others. When the Holy Spirit comes with tongues of fire at Pentecost, Mary is there, ready to bear Jesus out into the rest of the world, telling her story, which is his story, to all generations as they call her 'blessed'. There must have been a deep sense of recognition, of homecoming, as she encountered the Spirit of life again.

For reflection or discussion

Are you afraid that letting God further into your life will make you less yourself?

How do we celebrate our glorious individuality, the 'variety of gifts' of the one Spirit?

Lord, we pray for the gift of the Holy Spirit, that we may know our true selves in the life of the Son, your beloved. Amen.

28

Time and
eternity

Dreamtime Birth,
Greg Weatherby

Greg Weatherby's painting both is and is not the nativity of Jesus. There are clear, playful references to the gospel accounts – the three kingly figures kneeling at the crib, for example. But Weatherby also seems to be suggesting that there are eternal, universal motifs here. In particular, he is making connections between the Christian story of the birth of Jesus, and some of the aboriginal beliefs about the sacredness of the universe. The setting is obviously Australian, with sheep and oxen replaced with kangaroos and crocodiles, and in the background is Uluru, the sacred rock, associated with the creation of the world. It is tempting to see the two hands, pouring down light and blessing on the baby, who stretches his own arms upwards in delighted response, as a Trinitarian symbol; but the hands can also be seen as a depiction of the universal sense of gratitude at the provision of life, both at the beginning of all things and daily, in each new birth. The landscape is painted with the colours and patterns of Aboriginal skin painting, again making the deep connections between all of life: humans and earth are 'painted' in the same colours because they are intimately connected.

The painting is a meditation on profound themes that illuminate the gospel accounts. The genealogies in Matthew and Luke both suggest that the birth of Jesus links back to the meaning and purpose of the whole of creation, encouraging us to go back to the Genesis creation accounts, and see again that the world is created to be interconnected. Each 'day' of creation is built on the one before, and human beings are created to help all other created beings stay connected to their creator, through the

intimate and powerful human 'imaging' of the divine. Paul picks up universal creation themes when he calls Jesus the 'Second Adam'. If 'Adam' stands for all of human creation, then, in Jesus, humanity is being reborn, redefined. So there is no denying the universal themes in the birth of Jesus – they are essential to what is going on.

But the gospel accounts are also deeply resistant to a mythical reading, if that means that the universal reading could be divorced from the particularity of the story told. Matthew, Luke and Paul are making a claim about how the whole of creation and history finds its truth only through the existence of this particular person, Jesus Christ. It is not that Jesus is a useful carrier of themes of creation and rebirth that might exist independently of him. Instead, the New Testament suggests, it is only because the whole of creation is 'Jesus-shaped' from the very beginning that we are able to start recognizing meaning and purpose. It is not that the Son of God becomes incarnate in order to be like us, but that, through the Incarnation, we find ourselves in him: he is the original and we are the copies. It is not that we see that all of creation is interdependent and made for relationship, and then read that back into our understanding of the divine, but the other way round: God the Trinity is the relational reality from which the creation comes, and so all the connections of the universe come from the nature of God. The end result is similar – we and the whole of everything that is made are connected with each other and with God, and so there are consistent patterns of meaning that can be found in all attempts to articulate the reality of the world. It is just that the New Testament is insistent that this is innate to God, but not to us or the world.

Perhaps that sounds like typical Christian arrogance, with its claim to exclusive access to the truth. And Christians have certainly used their theology as a weapon rather than a vocation: it should be calling us to a way of living and relating to the world, not to a way of exerting dominance. But there is a logic to the understanding that it is only in this particular revelation in Jesus Christ that we find the coherence of all things. What Jesus lives out – from birth to death to resurrection and Ascension – is the unbreakable relationship of Father, Son and Holy Spirit, through and for which we are created. This is not an 'impersonal' thing, because relationships are not impersonal: it is offered by a person, Jesus, to each of us in our own individual personhood. We are not abstract universals to God, but as real and particular as Jesus. This is a deep and universal truth, but lived out only in and through particular people, like us.

For reflection or discussion

Do you feel you have a 'personal' relationship with God, which takes you, as you are, seriously?

What do you think it means to say that belief in Jesus Christ is a 'vocation'?

Heavenly Father, you love us with the love that is poured out in your Son, Jesus Christ; through the power of the Spirit, help us to trust that you can see us in truth and yet still love us. Amen.

29

The adoration of the magi

The Adoration of the Magi, c.1501–6, Francisco Henriques and Vasco Fernandes (Grão Vasco)

Francisco Henriques and Grão Vasco show us the contrast between the strange visitors and the Virgin and Child. The visitors are exotic, richly and extravagantly dressed. The beautiful white, tasselled boots of the magus at the left of the picture are hardly sensible wear for long-distance travel, but presumably he has others to worry about keeping them clean. The middle figure flaunts his plumed crown, and he wears bands of gold at his wrists and ankles; he has no interest in appearing inconspicuous. The older man, kneeling to worship the baby, has a rich, warm cloak and his beard and hair look freshly coiffed. No wonder they went first to Herod's palace, so obviously their natural habitat.

By contrast, the baby is entirely naked, while Mary is dressed in simple, unornamented black, with her head bare, and her hair in school-girlish plaits. She is sitting outside her temporary home, a stable that has seen better days, its roof decaying. The donkey in the background shows no interest in the visitors, but continues to munch from the sparse foliage of the tree against which Mary is leaning. The elaborate gold and ebony containers seem wholly out of place in this scene. Very reluctantly, Mary is taking the costly jar in one hand, as though it is the last thing in the world that a young mother wants. Her face suggests that she knows the symbolism of the gifts and does not appreciate being reminded of it.

Yet the painters also show that the still figures of the Virgin and Child are the centre of authority in the picture. It is not just that the old man is kneeling before the naked child, with his

hands clasped in prayer; his companions, too, are awed and uncertain in this presence. The man on the left of the picture lifts his hat, acknowledging that here is someone greater than himself, and the central, dark-skinned figure is standing with his legs awkwardly splayed, as though uncertain whether or not to join the kneeling figure. They know they have come to the right place, however unexpected it looks, but they are not quite sure of the social etiquette in such strange circumstances. It should be Mary, the young peasant girl, and Jesus, the vulnerable infant, who are off-balance, but instead it is the wealthy and mighty visitors. This is a new world they are entering, but it is one where the child and mother are completely at home.

Matthew's Gospel is the only one to mention the magi, who are often politely described as 'wise men', but whose wisdom probably derived from the almost occult science of divination using the stars, a bit like astrology. They must have been good at it, too, if their wealth and status are anything to go by. But that world, the world of government by dark and impersonal forces, is to meet its match in the just and generous rule of the new king whom they have come to worship. They are the first to give up everything to follow Jesus Christ. Their submission to the new ruler is clear in this poignant painting, as in the Gospels.

Yet God does not despise the skill that brought them here. They used all the gifts and tools they had and came to the Christ Child, to lay it all at his feet. Their passionate commitment to their profession made them the first witnesses from among the Gentiles, the first to signal that this birth is for all, not just for the insiders. Matthew does not actually say that there were only three magi – we infer that from the three gifts – but he does tell us that they came 'from the East', from outside, and were 'overwhelmed with joy' (Matthew 2.10) when they reached their destination. The star that guides the magi to Jesus is visible to all, though not all take any notice of it. When Joseph dreams (Matthew 1.20, 2.19), the gospel tells us that he is directed by an angel of the Lord. When the magi dream (Matthew 2.12), there is no specific mention of an angel, and yet the end result is still directed by God. Subtly, Matthew is telling us something about God: God makes and guides and loves everything, not just those who know it.

For reflection or discussion

Are there gifts and skills that you have been made to feel are not 'Christian'? If so, what, and why?

What should our attitude be to those of other faiths?

Lord of all truth, give us the Spirit of discernment, that we may see the likeness of Jesus Christ in all the many and varied gifts you bestow on all whom you have made. Amen.

30

Mother and Child

*Mother Mary and
Child Christ*, mid
eighteenth century,
late Mughal,
Muhammad Shah
period

This lovely painting of the visit of the magi to Mary and Jesus shows something of the universal appeal of the Mother and Child. The Mughal artist has carefully given some local colour, while not entirely locating the group. The figures are set against a building with the pierced and inlaid decorative style so familiar from the grandeur of the Taj Mahal, and although this house is on a much smaller scale, it does suggest that Mary has moved upmarket in the imagination of this painter. This is no stable, and Mary is as richly dressed as her visitors, suggesting more a meeting of equals than Matthew's Gospel would imply. Mary's halo, too, is jewelled and glowing, and she is clearly the centre of this picture. Islam has a great reverence for Mary, and the early Christian missionaries to Mughal India were startled at the interest and respect shown to the Mother and Child.

Devotion to Mary started early in Christian piety. A fourth-century bishop got himself into hot water by quibbling about her title, 'the God-bearer'. Although Nestorius and his opponents had genuine theological nuances to debate, there is no doubt that Mary's popularity in the prayers of the ordinary Christians of the day also played its part in the decision that Nestorius had got it wrong, and that Mary is, indeed, the one who brings God to birth in history.

Mary is a symbol of the human response to God and she is the mother of all Christians, the first among equals in the company of those who say yes to God through Jesus Christ. Mary welcomes the Holy Spirit, and so she is the first to allow

the Holy Spirit to make her life Jesus-shaped. In Mary's case, that is a physical thing as well as a spiritual one: the baby grows inside her, distending her belly, pressing on the walls of her skin, literally filling her. For those of us who come after, there will certainly be material consequences if we say yes to the Holy Spirit: Jesus Christ will come and live in us, and our lives will take their shape from him more and more, as he turns us towards his Father in love and obedience.

But perhaps this painting, like the myriad paintings of the Mother and Child, also suggests a certain hunger that Mary should represent not just all Christians, but women in particular. Between the Father and the Son, such gendered terms, and the ungendered Holy Spirit, is there a place for women? Yet we profoundly misunderstand the Incarnation if we concentrate on Jesus' masculinity. For the Christians of the first few centuries, the emphasis on Mary's role is not because she is a woman in a man's world, but because her story tells us that Jesus is really born, as we all are, and is subject to the same dangers and vulnerabilities that we all are. The Son of God does not bypass the usual means of entry into the world, any more than he bypasses the usual means of exit: he is really born and he really dies, to be with us.

Mary tells us that Jesus is truly human, as we are, whatever our gender. God does not need to come again as a woman to pour God's vitality and love into every part of the human family – that is done in Jesus Christ. In the season of Epiphany, we see the gospel story reaching out beyond the stable, beyond Bethlehem and Jerusalem, beyond the chosen people of God, to the whole world. But we also see its meaning getting larger and larger, more and more inclusive: here come wise men from afar, who know nothing of Israel's God, and yet know enough to come and worship; they invite us to find ourselves, too, at the cradle, where meanings shift and are made new.

Jesus comes to break down the dividing walls between different stories of the world – Jewish and Gentile, slave and free, male and female. Jesus brings all of us into a new humanity, defined not by separation but by invitation, into God's family. More fundamental than any of the ways in which we define and separate humanity is God's definition – in Jesus Christ, humanity is loved, affirmed and welcomed. Epiphany means 'showing', 'revelation', and this is a vital moment of clarity for us as men and women – in Jesus Christ, we have a common humanity. From that certainty, we can explore difference as a gift, drawing us closer, not driving us apart.

For reflection or discussion

Is God 'masculine' in your prayers? If so, what effect do you think that has on your relationship with God?

What does your church family reflect about the relationships between women and men?

Lord, pour out your Holy Spirit on us, so that we may shape our lives into the likeness of Jesus Christ, and bring to birth, in word and deed, the new humanity where all are welcomed and seen in truth and love. Amen.

31

The conversion of Paul

Conversion of Saint Paul, 1601, Michelangelo Merisi da Caravaggio

Caravaggio's extraordinary picture is a study in strange perspectives. It shows the moment when Paul, on the Damascus road, on his way to persecute the fledgling Christian community, is struck from his horse and blinded by the power of his encounter with the Risen Jesus. The full story is in Acts 9, and then Paul tells it again in Acts 26, as part of his defence when he is brought to trial before King Agrippa. He also alludes to it in his letter to the Galatians, though with less detail (Galatians 1.13–16). This is such a significant story that it bears repetition, particularly in Epiphany. Paul's ministry is one of the key moments when the Christian faith crosses a boundary and breaks out into new territory, since Paul's calling is to be the 'Apostle to the Gentiles'.

It is ironic that this illumination of the reach of the good news should start with a blinding. Paul has to let go of all that he 'saw' and understood, before he can 'see' his way forward along the new path. This is the moment Caravaggio paints for us. The bewildering perspective is not just a bit of painterly boasting, demonstrating Caravaggio's mastery, but a depiction of the total disorientation that Paul is experiencing. He lies helpless, in disarray and in danger of being trampled by his panic-stricken horse, but all of that has faded into unreality. His face looks strangely peaceful and his arms reach up, as though to embrace the force that has unseated him. Paul's servant is standing in the shadows, which is the natural light of the time of day and the road they are on. The light that shines on Paul, bringing out the colours of his skin and his cloak, is the light of Christ, and it is

clear that the servant cannot see it; his only concern is to try to calm the frightened horse.

In both accounts of this incident in Acts, Paul hears the voice of Jesus, who asks him to explain his driving anger against the Christian Church. Strikingly, Jesus identifies the Church with himself, and asks Paul, 'Why are you persecuting me?' Later, when Paul has travelled far and wide, proclaiming the good news of Jesus Christ, one of the metaphors he regularly uses for Christians is 'the body of Christ' (Romans 12.5; 1 Corinthians 10.16, 17, 12.12, 13, 18, 25, 27; Ephesians 1.23, 2.16, 3.6, 4.4, 12, 16, 5.30; Colossians 1.18, 2.17, 19, 3.15). Did this understanding spring from his very first encounter with Jesus, here on the Damascus road?

The second time Paul tells this story in Acts, he adds a further detail: Jesus also said to him, 'It hurts you to kick against the goads' (Acts 26.14). Perhaps that is what Paul had just been doing to his horse, in his furious anger against the Christians, trying to force his resisting horse along faster. By the time Paul tells King Agrippa what happened to him, he has had time to reflect on the encounter, time to live out his changed understanding. He can see the force of Jesus' metaphor, and look back on his old self, wilfully heading in the wrong direction, causing pain and damage to himself, as he tried to fight against Jesus. By now, Paul has been travelling along the right road, the way meant for him, and he can look back with compassionate understanding at that angry and uncomprehending self. He had to be 'converted', made to turn on to a different pathway, so that he could find himself again.

When Paul ceased to 'kick against the goads', that did not mean that his life became easy and peaceful. He tells us in

2 Corinthians 6.4–5 about some of the consequences of his change of direction, like 'beatings, imprisonments, riots, labours, sleepless nights, hunger'. But he writes about these almost as though they are external and not very relevant; what hurts him is when he feels that the Corinthians have separated themselves from him in some way, when he feels that he no longer has their affection. He has so internalized that profound theological insight from his first encounter with Jesus on the road to Damascus – Jesus' people are part of Jesus – that he cannot bear the thought of divisions between Christians.

So Paul shines the light of his conversion into our Epiphany season, and calls us to unity with the one who was born so that he could share our lives and we could share his.

For reflection or discussion

Are you 'kicking against the goads' of what you are called to be and do?

Can you identify a moment, and continuing moments, of 'conversion'?

Lord of light, shine the pure light of truth on the path that leads us to Jesus Christ, and may we walk in the power of the Spirit, with all your children, towards our home in you. Amen.

32

Simeon
and Anna

Simeon's Song of
Praise, c.1700,
Arent de Gelder

As shown by the witnesses to Jesus' birth, and the first Epiphany encounters, God's strategy is very strange. The angels go to all the trouble of summoning shepherds to see the baby in the manger, and we are told that all who heard the shepherds' story later were 'amazed' (Luke 2.18). It sounds a bit like the pub story of the fisherman boasting of a gigantic fish: how convinced were the 'amazed' listeners, and what did they do about it? Next, God arranges a star, which, for all its visibility and light, seems to have been designed to bring three strange and distinctly unorthodox wizards to visit the baby. When they returned home by another route (Matthew 2.12), what did they do with their newfound knowledge? Even if they shared it, the family had fled for safety to Egypt, so no one else would be able to follow up the wise men's story.

The next odd witnesses of God's arrival on earth to save all people are Simeon and Anna. As Jesus' parents take him to the Temple for the usual ritual purification, they encounter these two elderly strangers, who, like the wise men and the shepherds, seem to have been specially selected by God, and instantly recognize what they are seeing.

Although we are not told how old Simeon is, his response when he sees Jesus suggests that he knows his death is now close, and welcome, since his life's purpose is fulfilled. 'Master, now you are dismissing your servant in peace,' he says, with joy (Luke 2.29). This is the moment that de Gelder paints, as Simeon gazes upwards in ecstasy. He holds the baby, while

Anna stands praying beside the bundled-up child. We do know Anna's age; Luke tells us that she is 84, a very great age in that period. He also tells us that, like Simeon, she has dedicated her life to God, having been widowed at an early age. Around the group there are shadows, so the light that reflects on Simeon's upturned face and Anna's lowered one comes from the child, 'the light to lighten the Gentiles', as Simeon calls him, the light of the world.

The coverings that de Gelder has painted for the child have a strange, bright-red splodge in the middle. It may be a reference to Jesus' future death, but it looks almost as though the child has given birth to the two old people standing on either side of him. Perhaps it can even symbolize both at once, as Jesus' death and resurrection are the gateway to the eternal life that Simeon and Anna expect.

Like the shepherds and the wise men, Simeon and Anna are not strategic witnesses to the coming of the Messiah. Although both are clearly known in their community for their holiness and their spiritual discernment, their time is short, and not many will see the baby through their eyes.

De Gelder helps us to see why that does not matter. The child is his own illumination; light pours out from him. Yet God chooses that the first witnesses of his mighty act of salvation shall be the marginalized, the poor, the unorthodox and the old. This is the nature of God's kingdom: it belongs to the poor, the meek, the merciful and those who, like Simeon and Anna, can see past the trappings of worldly kingship to the true God who has come to set his people free.

God does not choose the wealthy, the powerful or the successful to parent the Son, or to be his witnesses, because they would be in danger of misrepresenting the kingdom to fit their own success. Instead, God grows his kingdom gently, one person at a time, but with the inexorable power of resurrection life. From the testimony of shepherds and magi, and, later, the fishermen and tax collectors, outcast women and healed sinners, the good news that God is with us has spread over all the earth. Those of us who pass on the message now need to be careful that we understand the nature of this good news and do not make it in our own likeness. We need to test our hearts and our eyes: would we rejoice, like Simeon and Anna, at God, present in a helpless child, with no achievements to its name? Would we see the light that lightens the Gentiles, and rejoice? It is time to learn again from the witnesses that God invites to the birth of the Son.

For reflection or discussion

Who are the people in your life to whom you long to present Jesus?

Do we make enough space in the life of the Church to hear the witness of the older members of our congregations?

Lord, present your Son, Jesus Christ, to us in the temples of our hearts and lives, and then send us out in the power of the Spirit to witness to your strange and glorious kingdom. Amen.

33
God and suffering

Salome with the Head of St John the Baptist, c.1570, Titian

From the beginning, the coming of Jesus into his world as saviour and king is, ironically, accompanied by violence. Matthew's Gospel tells of the murderous rage of King Herod when he hears of a potential threat to his power (Matthew 2). The wise men, innocently seeking the new king, not surprisingly head first of all for the royal court. They alone, of all the people who must have seen the star, discern what it purports and follow it, but then, at the last moment, their clarity and ability to see beyond the surface deserts them, and they allow their own assumptions to get in the way of their attention to the star. The consequences of that momentary lapse are terrible. Herod is alerted to the possibility of another king and, when he cannot get the wise men to betray what they discover, he indiscriminately kills all children under two, in and around Bethlehem, just to be on the safe side.

It is another member of the Herod family who is responsible for the death of John the Baptist. Titian paints Herod's step-daughter, Salome, who has tricked Herod into executing John, rather than lose face in front of his friends (see Matthew 14). The expression on Salome's face is a mixture of delight at the discovery of her own power and disgust at the sight of the severed head. The young serving woman and the little black slave boy are in shadow, out of the light of the triumph that blazes from Salome. They are learning a bitter lesson about her power, too: if she can demand the head of the feared and celebrated prophet, John the Baptist, then what chance have they, if her deadly whim falls on them? John's head, drained of

all colour, and the faces of the two servants, equally darkened, seem to belong together: they are the dispensable ones. John has served his purpose; he has announced the coming of the Messiah and has baptized Jesus for his ministry, and now he is finished. Despite the angelic announcement of his birth and the success of his ministry, he is not the heart of the story, any more than the two servants are.

It is easy to feel that this is God's fault. Surely God permits far too much collateral damage in all the great divine actions, from creation onwards. Ivan Karamazov, in Dostoevsky's great novel, speaks for generations of hurt and angry human beings, as he 'respectfully returns his ticket' to God – the price is too high; if the act of creation costs the suffering of one innocent child, then creation is too expensive, Ivan decides. It is not God who carries out these atrocities: it is one Herod who slaughters the children of Bethlehem and another who sacrifices John the Baptist to the whim of a pretty girl; it is human tyranny and wickedness that leads to all the tragic and terrible suffering in the world, just as it is human indifference and brutality that hammers the nails into the agonized flesh of Jesus on the cross. But it is still God's world.

The 'problem of evil' and of innocent suffering is particular to a theology that speaks of God as good, loving and powerful, and so cannot explain the existence of evil. If God is not good, or not powerful, then human beings must still endure suffering, but they do not need to lay it at God's door. Since it is a problem most acutely felt by our understanding of God, perhaps it is the one that God is calling us to live in and with. When God the Son comes to live with us, in Jesus Christ, the problem is at the heart of his interaction with us. He is born as a vulnerable baby, whose birth provokes the mad anger of a tyrant, and he dies, abandoned by friends, disposed of as a nuisance by religious and secular authority. God's action in Jesus seems to exacerbate the problem, rather than ease it.

Watching Jesus, we see him constantly redefining how the world must be and where its truth and heart lie. The poor, the sick, the needy, the outcast, the powerless, those at the centre of the 'problem of evil' are the ones Jesus attends to, and he calls on us to do the same. A different order is possible, but do we want it?

For reflection or discussion

Where has the 'problem of evil' touched your own life, and how has that made you feel about God?

What would it look like for us to live faithfully attending to the ones who are most affected by the 'problem of evil'?

Lord Jesus Christ, you lived and died as a man of sorrows, acquainted with grief: give us the Spirit of compassion for those who suffer and the Spirit of courage to fight against injustice, for the glory of the Father. Amen.

34
The baptism of Jesus

The Baptism of Christ, 1450, Piero della Francesca

According to Matthew, Mark and Luke, Jesus' baptism marks the beginning of his public ministry. So far, preparing for Epiphany, others have witnessed to what Jesus will mean for the world, from the wise men to Simeon and Anna; now, at last, Jesus himself steps into the limelight. His baptism is a statement about identity and commitment, about affirmation and acceptance, offered to Jesus and by him.

Piero della Francesca's painting of this moment is full of symbolism, each detail building up to the revelation of who Jesus is and what he must do. On the left of the painting stand the three angels who visited Abraham and Sarah (Genesis 18) to offer a promise of God's faithful love, to be shown in the conception of a son, Isaac. Isaac is a sign that God's love and God's promises never fail – they go on from one generation to another. The three angels are here to witness to the fact that, in Jesus, God's promise is to be fulfilled, not just partially, for Abraham and his bloodline, but fully, for all humanity. The three angels are dressed in rich, clear colours, but they stand in the shade, seen only by us. They are caught between two trees – their own, where they sheltered from the heat outside Abraham's tent, and Jesus' tree, which is both the Eden tree and the fatal tree of the cross. Jesus will become the terrible fruit of this tree, so that when we eat his body and drink his blood, his obedience displaces our human disobedience, the disobedience of 'Adam'. In the background of the picture there is someone stripping off his outer garments, waiting to step into the new clothing, the new life that Jesus is preparing.

Next to Jesus, John is pouring the water of baptism over Jesus' head. His free hand and the angle of his feet show that he is not comfortable about this; he knows that Jesus does not need to repent and be cleansed, and that any ministry should be going in the other direction.

John's feet have another message, too. John is standing with one foot in each world; one on the bank and one on the Way, with Jesus. John's job is to point to Jesus, not to walk the path himself. But if the path is Jesus' journey to the cross, then John, too, is walking a path to death at the hands of Herod. Jesus himself is standing firmly on the Way, the path that leads through his death to our life. Jesus' followers became known as the ones who walked the Way, following Jesus, the only guide who knows how to navigate this path. At his baptism, Jesus accepts that this is his path, for our sake. He identifies with us and commits himself to be with us and for us. Identity and commitment. For us, baptism admits the reality of sin, from which we need to be cleansed. Jesus, too, admits the reality of sin, and although he does not need to be cleansed, he will enter into the terror and brokenness of the sinful world to be with us and to lead us home.

If the picture shows us Jesus' identification with us and commitment to us, his affirmation and his love and acceptance of us, the heart of the picture shows us that this is also the Father's action. The dove, the symbol of the Holy Spirit, hovers over Jesus' head. As Jesus offers us his love and solidarity, so the dove offers Jesus the Father's affirmation and identification. 'This is my beloved Son,' the Father declares. The movement of love from Jesus to us flows down from God the Father and the Holy Spirit. God has not sent Jesus off on an errand into enemy territory; instead, in Jesus, God has come to reclaim creation, in an act of such faithfulness and love that nothing will be able to stop it, not even death.

Jesus begins his public ministry from this moment of baptism, with words of love and commitment ringing in his ears, affirming his identity. What Jesus receives is what he passes on: we find our identity as beloved children in him. What Piero della Francesca shows us is the beneficent flow of God's mercy and love, flowing from Jesus to us, and for us, in our turn, to pass on to others. The reversal of the flood, the beginning of new life.

For reflection or discussion

Who or what affirms you as a beloved child of God? Who or what tries to undermine that?

Do you think that we should revive 'the Way' as the description of discipleship as a journey?

Lord, as you declared your love for us in Jesus Christ, send your Holy Spirit to renew in us the Spirit of sonship, so that today we may walk the Way, rejoicing. Amen.

35

Prefiguring death

The Anointing of Christ, 2009, Julia Stankova

The sombre note sounds throughout this season. Even as the angels sing, the wise men journey and the faithful who have waited for so long rejoice, there is the evidence of the myrrh, the sword that will pierce Mary's heart and the murderous rage of Herod. We watch and realize that, because God will use only the power of life and love, the powers of death and hate will be out in force, determined to defend their bitter reign. The disciples do not understand that this kind of power can never be beaten using any weapon other than the divine one of constant, faithful refusal to become full of hate or fear. This is the secret of God: nothing can ever make God act in a way that is false to the divine nature. In our world, this looks like weakness, because we have so accepted ungodly definitions of power. Yet as we watch Jesus heal the sick, love the unloved, and go into death and out the other side, we begin to get a glimpse of a reality so enormous, so beyond anything we can conceive, the reality of God, so powerful that God can live in what God has made and still be unchangingly faithful to the divine nature.

The disciples are not alone in their incomprehension. We who call ourselves disciples of Christ still do not really trust that God knows how to behave, and that God's power is sufficient. Julia Stankova paints a moment in the Gospels where someone, just for an instant, shows herself to be in tune with Jesus' mission. In all four Gospels the incident occurs at a time when the likelihood of Jesus' death comes closer. In Mark 14, Matthew 26 and John 12, the anointing happens as part of the build-up of anger from those around Jesus. In Matthew and Mark, the

woman is not named, but is described as 'sinful'; in John, if this is the same incident, she is named as Mary of Bethany, sister of Lazarus, the man Jesus raised from the dead. In Luke, the incident is placed much earlier in Jesus' ministry, just after he has heard of the death of John the Baptist. John is Jesus' relative and witness, one of the few who understand him, so there is personal grief for Jesus, but there is also a sign of the callous brutality of the regime under which Jesus himself will die.

While the disciples are often found trying to talk Jesus out of his strange belief that the Messiah must die, this woman, with her act of costly, humiliating and apparently pointless love, demonstrates that she has understood the even more costly, humiliating and painful act that Jesus will undertake on the cross; she has understood the true nature of the power that is love.

Stankova paints the expression of dedication on the woman's face: she is oblivious to everything but this sacrificial act. She does not care about the three people looking at her with a mixture of excitement, prurience and disdain – their attitude is their own problem, not hers. There is sensuality in this act, as shown in the deep-red colouring, and in the luscious smoothness of the woman's hair lying on Jesus' feet, but it is more the gentle physicality of a mother washing her baby than anything sexual. The painter deliberately chooses that we do not see Jesus' face: there is almost something impersonal about the way in which the woman approaches her sacrificial act, with her eyes closed, her hands not reaching out to touch. Jesus understands this: he tells her that it is as though she is taking care of his dead body. Of all the people who come to Jesus, in hope, in anger, in fear, in need, she alone comes simply to serve; she alone accepts that this is the way of love in the broken world; she alone affirms that Jesus is doing the will of God in preparing to die. What comfort it must have been to him, to have one other human being understand this deep and terrible truth. It is bitterly ironic that the first witnesses so confused this story that we are not sure when it happened or who the woman was. It is not until after Jesus' death and resurrection that the prescience of this act becomes clear, and we are still trying to understand it to this day.

For reflection or discussion

What are the most important things or people in your life, for which, or for whom, you might be willing to make great sacrifices?

In what ways might we serve our communities and help them to grow in care for the vulnerable and the needy?

Almighty God, teach us the invincibility of your faithful love and, with the help of the Holy Spirit, lead us to Jesus Christ, and to those whom he died to serve. Amen.

36

The
wedding at
Cana

*The Wedding at
Cana*, 1562–3, Paolo
Veronese

In John's Gospel, the wedding at Cana of Galilee is the 'epiphany' moment. John calls this the first of Jesus' signs, the moment at which the disciples 'believed in him' (John 2.11). In Veronese's crowded, anachronistic picture of the occasion, while the other guests at the wedding are busily chatting, eating and listening to the music, Jesus looks out of the canvas at us, asking us if we, too, now believe.

Veronese has set the scene in the Venetian society of his own day; Jesus and the disciples are wearing stereotypical New Testament clothes, but everyone else is dressed in the height of Venetian fashion, and they are surrounded by classical architecture. Many of the faces would have been recognisable to the cognoscenti, and it is generally accepted that Veronese painted himself into the picture, as the musician wearing white, in the foreground. This is very much a celebration, but it is clear that it is Jesus' banquet – it is he, rather than the wedding couple, who sits at the centre of the table. Above him is a lamb being butchered, ready to be cooked to feed the guests, but also making the connection between this feast, the Last Supper and eucharistic feast. Meals play a central role in Jesus' life and teaching, always as a symbol of gathering people to God's family table, through Jesus' costly work of making this world, its life and its death, his home. Here, at Cana, the work begins: Jesus, the guest, becomes the host.

The story that John tells of this wedding is an enigmatic one. The bride and groom are incidental – we never meet the bride, and the groom features only very briefly. The action is between

Jesus and his mother, Jesus and a servant, and Jesus and his disciples. At no point does John explain anything: what does the exchange between Jesus and his mother mean, for example? The amount of wine Jesus produces is ludicrously exaggerated, but the steward who compliments the bridegroom on the quality does not know who is responsible for it. Only the servant who witnessed the miracle, Mary and the disciples know anything. It is like a prefiguring of the much bigger miracle of the resurrection, so startling and yet still witnessed by only a few. John seems to be suggesting that connection, introducing the story of the wedding with the words 'on the third day' (John 2.1).

John calls this glorious, generous miracle a 'sign', the first of the seven that occur in the main body of John's Gospel. They include three healings, the feeding of the 5,000, Jesus walking on the water, and the raising of Lazarus. But this first one is the most mysterious, the least necessary, the most simply and spontaneously joyful. The worst that would have happened without this miracle is that the bridegroom's family might have lost face, and the guests might have got less drunk. Why is this an 'epiphany', a revelation, a showing to the world of who Jesus is?

Perhaps the 'third day' may give us a clue? John begins the Gospel with a retelling of the creation of the world, with the word, the Son of God, as its heart and about to enter the world that was made through him and that will not recognize its maker. On the third day of God's creative work in Genesis 1, God creates the fruitful dry land, with all its plants and trees, its lush vegetation of every kind. And here in John's Gospel, on the third day, Jesus creates an abundance of fruitfulness again, this time in the form of the overflowing wine pots. What the disciples see is the generous, exuberant creativity of God at work again, in

Jesus. Just as God does not 'need' the world in order to be God, so Jesus does not 'need' to make gallons of wine; at the heart of the universe is the extravagant outpouring of God's love.

It is that same generosity and creativity, that same mastery of creation, that flow out of the other 'signs' that Jesus performs; they are signs that life flows from Jesus now, as it flowed through the Son at the beginning of the world. If few see or understand, that cannot diminish the truth. God is the source of all life, whether we know it or not, and, in Jesus, God offers us this life, without stint, leading into eternity.

For reflection or discussion

What 'signs' do you look back to in your life that help you believe in Jesus?

Is your church good at exuberant celebration, as a 'sign' of the life of God?

Lord of all joy, as you made a celebration at the wedding in Cana, so send on us your Spirit of overflowing love, that we may help each other to celebrate Jesus Christ, our redeemer. Amen.

37
The Church

Trinity – After Rublev, 2016, Meg Wroe

In Epiphany, we celebrate the ways in which Jesus is shown to the world. We, God's people, the Church, are among the ways in which God chooses to make the Son known. That seems a strange choice, given our stupidity and failures, but it is essential to what God is doing in Jesus. God does not save human beings in spite of themselves, or without their consent and co-operation, because the whole point of salvation is that we human creatures are invited into the life of God, as children, sisters and brothers of the Son. If God overrules us and forces us to be saved, then God negates the very meaning of creation and is no longer faithful to his own purposes, and so to the divine nature. The Church is the beginning of the new creation, where all whom God has called into life belong in one race, the humanity that knows itself to be God's beloved.

Meg Wroe's reimagining of Rublev's famous icon of the Trinity challenges the Church to step into its truth. Rublev showed a double vision, which was both the three angels who visited Abraham and promised that he and Sarah would have a son, and, at the same time, the Holy Trinity, promising us, too, that God is to be trusted. The thee angels were fed by Abraham, but the Trinity invite us to sit at their table, in the space left for us, the space we occupy as we stand in front of the painted table.

Wroe's painting is also a double vision: here we have Rublev's Trinity, inviting us in, but inviting us in all our particularity. In this painting, the three angels have real faces because the people whom God invites are not just 'humanity' in a generic sense,

but real, individual people. When God the Son becomes human, Jesus Christ is a real human being, who lives a particular life, in a one place, at a moment in history. It is precisely because he is genuinely human that what he does has universal significance. God affirms the reality and belovedness of each person. It is not just that God, in a Lordly kind of way, bestows a general blessing on the human race, but that God becomes human, in the only way it is possible to be human, as an individual. And so it is with the Church: it cannot have any universal meaning if it is not full of actual people. The Church is not collective humanity, but every individual, bringing their own peculiar gifts, for the enrichment of the whole. The Church needs to imitate God in this, as in all things, and beware of making vast statements about the generality of humankind, which risk leaving particular people behind.

This, too, Wroe signals in her icon. Her Trinity are black and minority ethnic, unlike most of the people in the paintings in the rest of this book. One of the wise men is usually portrayed as black, and that is partly to emphasize the exotic foreignness of these visitors, and partly to pick up the great theme that all are invited to the cradle of God with us. But, on the whole, the art and iconography of the Church has not represented the full particularity of human beings, but has narrowed the range down to people in the image of the artist. Wroe's challenge to the Church is to recover its own theology and let it shine out in every depiction of the Church.

Our gift and calling as Church are not that we are good where others are not, or that we have had the sense to know God where others have not, but that God has called us to be a sign and a foretaste of the coming kingdom, where all human beings recover their relatedness to each other, because they have been adopted by God. For all its failures and active faults, the Church has still, miraculously, almost in spite of itself, spread the good news that God has come to make a home in every nation under the sun, and belongs equally in every place and in every heart. There is no 'typical' Christian, no favoured race or class or gender, all are invited to the table. When we make our sense of Church too small, so that it is more like a club for people like ourselves, then we have lost the vital heart of our calling, to proclaim that God was in Christ, reconciling the world to himself.

For reflection or discussion

Do you have an instinctive, unexamined picture of God? If so, does it need expanding?

Does your church represent the diversity of the community it is in, or is it more like an exclusive club?

Lord of all, enlarge our vision so that we see in all people the likeness of Christ. Send your Holy Spirit to teach us to pray together, 'Our Father', and then send us to live and work to your praise and glory. Amen.

COPYRIGHT ACKNOWLEDGEMENTS